THE WALTZ INVENTION

A PLAY IN THREE ACTS BY

VLADIMIR NABOKOV

PHAEDRA, 1966

Written in Russian by Vladimir Nabokov
(*September 1938, Cap d'Antibes*)

First Published in Russkie Zapiski (*November, 1938, Paris*)

Translation into English by Dmitri Nabokov (*Summer, 1964, Milan, Italy.*)

First Edition, February 1, 1966

Phaedra Inc.
220 East 42nd Street
New York 10017, N.Y.

to Véra

Foreword

Originally written in Russian, at the Cap d'Antibes on the French Riviera, in September 1938, this play, under the ambiguous title of *Izobretenie Val'sa*—which means not only "the invention of Vals (or Valse)", but also "the invention of the waltz"—appeared in November of the same year in *"Russkie Zapiski,"* an émigré review published in Paris. A Russian company planned its production there for the next season, and rehearsals, under Annenkov's talented direction, had started when World War Two put an end to the enterprise.

Readers of this somewhat belated translation should be made aware of two things: First, telethanasia, was in the Nineteen Thirties, a considerably less popular subject than it is today: in fact, certain passages (where my son and I have been especially careful not to disturb the old-fashioned folds of the original imagery) sound a prophetic, even doubly prophetic, forenote not only of the later atomystique, but of still later parodies of that theme—quite a record in its small dark way. And secondly, to spare modern readers unwarranted speculation, I wish to point out most emphatically that not only is there in my play no political "message" (to borrow a cant word from the jargon of quack reform) but that publication of its English version today has no topical import; nor would I have attempted to invent my poor Waltz today lest any part of me, even my shadow, even one shoulder of my shadow, might seem thereby to join in those "peace" demonstrations conducted by old knaves and young fools, the only result of which is to give the necessary peace of mind to ruthless schemers in Tomsk or Atomsk. It is hard, I submit, to loathe bloodshed, including war, more than I do, but it is still harder to exceed my loathing of the very nature of totalitarian states in which massacre is only an administrative detail.

The main revisions in the present text are based upon intentions more than a quarter of a century old, stemming as they do from the summer of 1939 (at Seytenex, Haute Savoie, and Frejus, Var) when, between butterfly hunting and moth luring, I was preparing the thing for the stage. To this category belong cuts in Waltz's blank-verse speech, new details concerning Perrault's death, an increased femininity in the Trance character, and the dialogue with Annabella in Act Two. Names have undergone alterations. "Waltz" has been chosen because it looks more cosmopolitan than "Valse" (but either way most of the pun is spun off). "Trance" was originally "*Son*," which means "dream" in Russian but would have got messed up with "son" and "sun" in an English transcription. The names of the eleven old generals (including three dummies) were Berg, Breg, Brig, Brug, Burg, Gerb, Grab, Grib, Gorb, Grob and Grub with untransmittable associations. They now all end in the phonetically weightier "ump" and present an analogous series of allusive sense.

Otherwise the translators have been as faithful to me as I would have liked them to be to any other playwright. A certain formality of phrasing, so typical of literary Russian when indulging a neutral prose rhythm (and so closely reproduced by the stiffish English of our choice) is here partly a structural device which aims at establishing the keenest possible contrast between those inhuman sentences and the poignant chaos over which they stalk.

If, from the very first, the action of the play is absurd, it is because this is the way mad Waltz—*before* the play starts— imagines it is going to be, while he waits outside, in a viking-style armchair—imagines the interview he has managed to wangle through old Gump and its fabulous consequences; an interview which in reality he is granted only in the last scene of the last act. As his waiting room dream unfolds, broken by intermissions of oblivion between the acts of his fancy, there occurs now and then a sudden thinning of the texture, a rubbed spot in the bright fabric, allowing the nether life to glimmer through. Why is he such a tragic figure? What upsets him so atrociously when he sees a toy on a table? Does it bring back his own childhood? Some bitter phase of that childhood? Not *his* childhood perhaps, but that of a child he has lost? What misfortunes, besides banal poverty, has he endured? What is the macabre and mysterious memory linked with Siberia, which a convict's dirge sung by a whore so strangely evokes? Who am I to propose such questions?

After the dreadful frustrations Freudians have experienced with my other books, I am sure they will refrain from inflicting upon Waltz a sublimation of the push-button power-feeling such as the manipulation of an elevator, up (erection!) and down (revenge suicide!). Neither can I do anything to please critics belonging to the good old school of "projected biography," who examine an author's work, which they do not understand, through the prism of his life, which they do not know. I have never craved political omnipotence, and Gump's daughter is five years older than Lolita.

When, sooner or later, *The Waltz Invention* sees the footlights and the black pit beyond, one hopes that whoever is going to produce it, and act in it, will take into account the poetry and the pathos underlying the bright demented dream. In contradistinction to the black pit of reality the scenery should be as rich and verisimilar as a Dutch painting. Please, no damned fire escapes, garbage cans, skeleton platforms with actors in overalls standing on different levels. I want what Waltz wanted—real carpets, crystal knobs on the doors, and those sculptured armchairs upholstered in golden leather that he liked so much (he does not mention them, but I know). And the uniforms of the eleven generals must be beautiful, must glow like Christmas trees.

Montreux
December 8, 1965   VLADIMIR NABOKOV

THE WALTZ INVENTION

Dramatis Personae

Salvator Waltz	a haggard inventor; a fellow author
The Minister of War	a gentle old man
Colonel Plump	his adviser, a balding fop
General Gump	Annabella's father; a middleman between the phenomenal and the fantastic
Myopic Bump	an official; a general; a chauffeur
Dump, a naturalized Ute	a janitor; a general; an architect and a cook
Hump, an undersized mute	a servant; a general and herald; a sports instructor
Corpulent Lump	an official; a general; a dentist
Red Mump	a reporter; a general; a physician
Intersexual Rump	a reporter; a general; a housekeeper
One-legged Stump	an official; a general; a gardener
Viola Trance	a reporter and Waltz's factotum; she is a smart woman of 30 in black masculine dress Shakespearean-masquerade style
Annabella Gump	a very pretty young girl, more or less real
Cleopatra	a courtesan
Olga	her sister
A Fat Girl	a Tsigan contralto
A Skinny Girl	a fancy pianist
An Old Blonde	a Bohemian poetess

The First and Third acts take place in the Office of the Minister of War; the Second, in the Council Hall of the Ministry. The action is situated in an imaginary country; the time is around 1935.

Act One

Office of the Minister of War. A window looks out on a cone-shaped mountain. Revealed, in strange attitudes, the Minister of War *and his secretary, the* Colonel.

- COLONEL

Bend your head back a little more. That will do. Stop blinking. Just a moment. . . . No, I can't see like this. Lean back some more. . . .

- MINISTER

I'm telling you it's under the upper lid, the *upper*—but you keep fishing under the lower.

- COLONEL

We shall look everywhere. Just one moment. . . .

- MINISTER

Much further to the left. . . . In the corner. . . . It hurts unbearably. Don't tell me you're incapable of turning up an eyelid.

- COLONEL

Here, give me your handkerchief. We'll have it out in a jiffy. . . .

- MINISTER

You are pulling my lashes off, damn you. Got it?

- COLONEL

Alas, I'm a city boy. No, the eyeball looks as clean to me as the white of a picnic egg. The speck must have gone but left a tiny sore.

5

- **MINISTER**

And I tell you it stings unbearably.

- **COLONEL**

I'll look once again, but I think it's your imagination.

- **MINISTER**

It's amazing what unpleasant hands you have. . . .

- **COLONEL**

Well, would you like me to try with my tongue?

- **MINISTER**

No, that's disgusting. Don't torture me.

- **COLONEL**

You know what? Change your position, then the light will be better. No, no, don't rub . . . one should never rub.

- **MINISTER**

Eh, wait a minute. . . . Yes, I actually think. . . . Yes, it's better!

- **COLONEL**

Ah, thank goodness.

- **MINISTER**

It's out. What a relief. Ah, bliss. (*Pause*) Well, what was it we were discussing?

- **COLONEL**

You were alarmed by the actions—

- **MINISTER**

Yes. I was, and am, alarmed by the actions of our unscrupulous neighbors. A nation of modest size, one would say, but how compact—all steel, a hedgehog of steel! The scoundrels invariably emphasize that they have the most amicable relations with us, while actually they do nothing but send us spies and mischief-makers. It's disgusting!

6

- COLONEL

Don't touch it any more if the pain's gone. Then, at home, you can apply something. Use boric acid, or, even better, a bit of cotton soaked in strong tea.

- MINISTER

No, it doesn't matter, it's all right now. Of course the whole damned matter will end in a thunderous row. The other members of the Cabinet don't care, but, as for me, I'll have to submit my resignation.

- COLONEL

Need I say that you are irreplaceable?

- MINISTER

Instead of the honey cakes of flattery, you ought to offer me the plain bread of sound advice. Ah, it's nearly eleven. There's no more business, I think. . . .

- COLONEL

Allow me to remind you that you have an appointment at eleven.

- MINISTER

I don't remember. Nonsense. Please leave those papers alone.

- COLONEL

Allow me to remind you once again that at eleven, on the recommendation of General Gump, you are to receive—

- MINISTER

General Gump is an old fogy.

- COLONEL

Here is his note, which you saw fit to answer in the affirmative. General Gump—

- MINISTER

General Gump is an old idiot.

- COLONEL

General Gump is sending you an inventor who has something important to communicate. His name is Salvator Waltz.

7

- **MINISTER**

What?

- **COLONEL**

A certain Salvator Waltz.

- **MINISTER**

One could dance to a name like that. All right. I suggest you see him in my place.

- **COLONEL**

That would accomplish nothing. I know these types, who invent a screw to replace the one missing in their head. He won't be satisfied until he gets to you even if it's across the dead bodies of your entire staff.

- **MINISTER**

Oh, you always find some excuse. Well, I guess this cup too I shall have to drink. Most likely he's already in the waiting room.

- **COLONEL**

Yes, these people are an impatient breed. It's like a messenger who runs many miles without pause to report a trifle, a dream, a chimera born of delirium. . . .

- **MINISTER**

And what is more, the General has already sent me some such characters. Remember the little old lady who invented the underwater lifeboat?

- **COLONEL** (*picking up the phone*)

To be carried by a submarine. Yes, I also remember that she subsequently sold her invention to another country.

- **MINISTER**

You remember all kinds of rubbish, don't you? Give me the phone. Well, is he here, what's his name . . . Silvio. . . . Silvio. . . ?

- **COLONEL**

Salvator Waltz.

8

- MINISTER (*into the phone*)

Yes, yes. . . . Send him in. (*to the Colonel*): Fools buy all sorts of things. The little old lady swindled *them*, but not me—no, sir: that's all there is to it. So she sold it. So what? For heaven's sake stop clenching your back teeth like that.

- COLONEL

I shall also need your signature on these papers.

- MINISTER

I'm upset, I'm irritated. Tomorrow the newspapers will be making a fuss over that spy business, and I'll have to listen to all kinds of claptrap. Incidentally, I'm not pleased with our official version. It should have been drawn up quite differently. . . .

(*Salvator Waltz enters*)

- WALTZ (*to the Colonel*)

Are you the War Minister?

- COLONEL

His Excellency the Minister is ready to see you.

- WALTZ

So it's not you, but (*to the Minister*) you.

- MINISTER

Take a seat. No, if you don't mind, not beside me but facing me.

(*Pause*)

- WALTZ

Ah—one can see the mountain perfectly from here.

- MINISTER

I have the pleasure of speaking to Mr. . . . . Mr. . . . . (to the Colonel) Where's that letter?

- COLONEL

Salvator Waltz.

- WALTZ

Well, you see, that's not quite exact. A chance pseudonym, fancy's bastard. As for my real name, you need not know it.

9

- MINISTER

Odd.

- WALTZ

Everything is odd in this world, Mr. Minister.

- MINISTER

Is that so? Anyway, the General writes me that you have something to communicate. A discovery, as I understand it?

- WALTZ

Once, in my early youth, a speck of something became lodged in my eye, with a quite unexpected result. For a whole month everything I saw was a beautiful pink, as if I were looking through the stained-glass windows of the church of St. Rose. The oculist who unfortunately cured me called it an optical glow. I am forty and a bachelor. I think those are all the biographical facts I dare give you.

- MINISTER

Curious. As I understand it, however, you came here on business?

- WALTZ

The formula "as I understand it"—which you have used twice already—is equivalent to an outright assertion of being right. I like precision of expression and detest circumlocutions, those hangnails of speech.

- COLONEL

Permit me to observe that it is exactly with circumlocutions that you are taking up the Minister's time. His Excellency is a very busy man.

- WALTZ (*to the Colonel*)

You really can't guess why my approach is so vague?

- COLONEL

No. Why?

10

• **WALTZ**

Because I object to your presence.

• **MINISTER**

Now, now, now. . . . You may speak quite freely in the presence of my secretary.

• **WALTZ**

But I should still prefer to deprive this room of his presence and talk with you in private.

• **COLONEL**

Deprive it! What insolence!

• **WALTZ**

Come, you won't impress me with—a play upon words. Private-deprived, indeed! I have two factories and a tenement house in Old Chestnut street, Punnington.

• **COLONEL** (*to Minister*)

Do you wish me to go?

• **MINISTER**

Oh well, if the gentleman. . . . if this gentleman makes it a condition. . . . (to Waltz): But I give you exactly ten minutes. (The Colonel leaves).

• **WALTZ**

Fine. I'll return them with interest, and probably even today.

• **MINISTER**

Your mode of expression is certainly rather arcane. As I understand it—that is, I mean to say, I'm told you are an inventor.

• **WALTZ**

A definition just as approximate as my name.

• **MINISTER**

All right, so it's approximate. Come on, I am listening.

• **WALTZ**

Yes, but I think you're not the only one. . . . (goes quickly to the door and opens it).

11

- COLONEL (*in the doorway*)

What a nuisance—I must have left here my cigarette case, a present from a beloved woman. Perhaps, though, I mislaid it in the washroom (*stumbles away*).

- MINISTER

Yes, yes, he's always mislaying women, I mean, things. Please, explain your business, I really don't have much time.

- WALTZ

I shall, with pleasure. I—or, rather, a devoted friend—has invented a certain machine. A fitting name for it might be "Telemort," or to keep it all Greek "Telethanasia." But that's too long.

- MINISTER

I see.

- WALTZ

By means of this device, which is as innocent in appearance as, say, a radio set, one can produce, at any distance, an explosion of incredible force. Is that clear?

- MINISTER

An explosion? I see.

- WALTZ

Mind you—at *any* distance: across continents, over a thousand and one dark seas. The number of such explosions is of course unlimited, and only a few minutes are necessary to prepare each one.

- MINISTER

Ah! I see, I see.

- WALTZ

My machine is kept far from here. Its whereabouts is veiled in utter, magical secrecy. But even allowing that by some vulgar chance someone were to come upon it, no one, in the first place, would be able to guess how to work it, and, secondly, another

12

one would immediately be built,—with awful consequences for the treasure hunters.

- MINISTER

Oh, I don't think anybody would try to steal such a thing.

- WALTZ

I must warn you, however, that I myself am totally unversed in technical matters, so that even if I so wished, I would be unable to explain the workings of my apparatus. It has been built by a cousin of mine, a gray-bearded man, also called Waltz, Walter Waltz, Walt Waltz, a genius, a super-genius! As for the business of calculating the locus, setting the thing correctly, and then pressing the button, it is true that I have learned that much. But to explain it—no, no, don't ask me. All I know comes down to one rather dim fact: two rays, or waves, have been discovered which, upon intersecting, cause an explosion one mile in radius. . . . I think it is one mile, in any case not less than that. All one has to do is to make them intersect at a given point on the globe. And that is all.

- MINISTER

Well, I'd say that was quite enough. You would not have brought blueprints with you, or something—the kind of description that comes with mechanical toys, build-it-yourself things, you know what I mean?

- WALTZ

Certainly not! What an absurd supposition.

- MINISTER

Sorry. I did not mean to offend you. On the contrary. And what is your field—you are not an engineer, then?

- WALTZ

In general I am a highly impatient man, as your secretary rightly observed. But for the present occasion I have laid in a supply of patience, and a certain part of this supply is still left. I shall say it once again: my apparatus is capable, by means of repeated

13

explosions, of annihilating and turning into a spread of smooth, glistening dust an entire city, an entire country, an entire continent.

• MINISTER

Oh, I believe you. Look here, you and I will have another chat about it some time. . . .

• WALTZ

Such a weapon gives its possessor power over the entire universe. It's so simple! Why on earth do you refuse to understand?

• MINISTER

No, not at all—I do understand. It's fascinating.

• WALTZ

That is all you can answer?

• MINISTER

Now don't get excited. You see. . . . Excuse me—A very annoying cough. Caught it at the last military inspection. . . .

(*the Colonel comes in*)

• WALTZ

You answer me with a cough? Is that it?

• MINISTER (*to the Colonel*)

Well, my friend, our inventor here has been relating wonders. I think we shall ask him to present a report. (*to Waltz*): But of course there's no hurry—we're up to our ears in reports.

• COLONEL

Yes, yes—do present a report.

• WALTZ (*to the Minister*)

Is this your last word?

• COLONEL

Your ten minutes are up, and His Excellency has many other tedious matters to attend to.

14

- WALTZ

Don't you dare talk to me of time! It is I who am in charge of time, and, if you want to know, you really do have little time left.

- MINISTER

There, we've had our chat, very glad to have met you, and now run along quietly, and some time we'll talk again.

- WALTZ

It's astounding, though! Imagine someone coming to a sailor's wife and saying: "I can see your husband's ship on the horizon." Don't tell me she won't tear off her apron and rush to have a look instead of asking the messenger to drop in on Wednesday with a report. Or imagine a farmer who learns in the middle of the night that his barn is on fire—don't tell me he won't go running out in his underwear. Or, when the victorious Field-marshal comes riding into a city he has captured, don't tell me the town mayor demands he present a petition if he wants to receive the keys to the city.

- MINISTER *(to the Colonel)*

I don't understand what he is talking about.

- COLONEL *(to Waltz)*

Please, go. Note has been taken of everything you've said, but now the audience is over.

- WALTZ

I am drawing on my last reserves of patience. Human language is the ideally precise tool nature has given us for instant communication of thought. Take advantage of this opportunity to understand. I am perfectly aware that when I present you with the proof of my power, you will pay much more attention to me. At first, though, I want to allow myself the luxury of mere speech, without visual aids and concrete threats. I ask you, deflect your intellect, give me access to it.—Elect intellect! Truly, my invention is worth that much!

15

- MINISTER (*rings*)

We have fully appreciated it; this is all highly interesting, but I have some urgent business. Afterwards, later on, I shall again be at your disposal.

(*The servant Hump comes in. He is dumb and uses sign language. To attract his master's attention, he shakes a rattle*).

- COLONEL (*to Hump*)

Please show Mr. Waltz out.

- WALTZ

Boor! At least allow me to finish my sentence.

- COLONEL

And you, kind sir, don't be rude!

- MINISTER

That's enough, that's enough.

- WALTZ

What a splendid view you have from the window! Take a look, before it is too late. (*Goes out*).

- MINISTER

How do you like that?

- COLONEL

Oh well, that's the cheapest kind of lunatic.

- MINISTER

Disgusting! From now on, I shall demand that all visitors undergo a preliminary psychiatric examination.

- COLONEL

I noticed at once that he was insane. One could even tell by his clothes. And those quick wild eyes.

- MINISTER

As to General Gump, I'll give him a good piece of my mind.

- COLONEL

I'll go take a look—I'm afraid he may be raving in the waiting room. (*Goes out*).

16

- MINISTER (*into the phone*)

I want General Gump. (*Pause*). Hello, General. Yes, it's me. How are you today? What? No, I asked how you were today. Yes, I know you have lumbago, but how is it—better? Oh well, in the spring all our little pains return. Who? No one has told me about it yet. Last night? What a shame! Thank goodness he died in his sleep, poor fellow. Yes, I'll send my colonel. Why, of course the widow deserves a pension. Only, my ministry doesn't handle that. I think they'll give it to her. What? But I'm telling you I'm not the one who decides these matters—I have absolutely nothing to do with it. Oh, good grief! All right, all right, I'll try. By the way, General, listen—I wanted to speak to you about your protégé, you know, that inventor you sent to me. Yes, that's just the point—he was here, and it turns out that he's just plain crazy. (*The Colonel comes in and puts a letter in the Minister's automatically outstretched hand*). Started spouting such nonsense that we practically had to throw him out of here. Invention, my foot! The old story about a fantastic machine that's supposed to produce explosions at a distance. Tell me, please—how did he ever get to you? Yes, yes, I know—and he got to the Major through someone else again. No, I'm not cross with you at all, but he made me lose a lot of valuable time and, besides, a character like that can murder one. Yes, yes, I understand all that, but still, you know, one has to be doubly careful. I must really beg you not to send me such freaks any more. And do get well in a hurry. Yes, it's very painful, I know. Fine, then. . . . give my best to your little Annabella. Oh, she's out horseback riding? Well, soon she'll be winning prizes, like her papa in his youth. No, I won't forget the widow. Well, au revoir, get well soon. (*To the Colonel*): What's this letter?

- COLONEL

You take a look. It's not devoid of interest.

- MINISTER

Listen, I can't read this. Never saw such handwriting. It's like a child's drawing of sea waves. Who is it from?

17

- COLONEL

Our madman gave it to me for you.

- MINISTER

Look here, this exceeds all limits. Please spare me.

- COLONEL

I must confess I deciphered it. Here, I'll read it to you. I assure you it's very amusing. "Mr. Minister, if our conversation had interested you more, the event I have planned would have been merely an illustration; now, however, it will serve as a warning. To put it briefly, I have au. . . . am. . . ." very illegible. Ah! ". . . . arranged with my assistant that exactly at noon, from that. . . . remote point where my device is kept, he will produce an explosion here and blow up the beautiful bi. . . . ben. . . ." This man's handwriting is really something! "the beautiful. . . ."

- MINISTER

Why waste your time figuring out pathological trash?

- COLONEL

"Blue" it must be. Yes, ". . . . the beautiful blue mountain that is so clearly visible from your window. Do not miss it—the effect will be remarkable. Yours, humbly waiting outside your office, Salvator Waltz."

- MINISTER

He really is quite a clown!

- COLONEL

You should have seen what a look he had when he gave it to me.

- MINISTER

Let's forget him. He'll wait a while and go. And naturally, if he ever comes back, tell him I'm not seeing anyone.

- COLONEL

Oh, of course.

- MINISTER

As for our good General, I gave him such a scolding over the phone that I think his gout is gone. By the way, you know who

18

died last night? Old Perrault—yes, yes. Seems only yesterday that he was reciting his wonderful fairy-tales at Christmas parties for disabled soldiers and at that wonderful mental home—what was its name—where your two cousins were interned. . . .

- COLONEL

Oh, very distant cousins. You were saying?

- MINISTER

Or am I thinking of the brothers Grimm? Well, no matter. I was saying?

- COLONEL

Funeral

- MINISTER

Ah yes. And remind me to talk to Ump tomorrow about a pension for the widow. It seems they were very badly off lately—it's a shame, I didn't even know.

- COLONEL

Oh well, that's the way it is. One man sinks, another drinks. I, for one, am always cheerful. Every day a new love affair.

- MINISTER

You gay dog, you!

- COLONEL

It's spring today, and the sun is warm. They're selling bunches of mimosas in the streets.

- MINISTER

Where are you having lunch today? Would you like to eat with me? There'll be steak with fried onion, ice cream. . . .

- COLONEL

Well, I can't refuse. But excuse me if I don't stay afterwards—a burning heart is stronger than heartburn.

- MINISTER

I'll excuse you. Ah—ten to twelve.

19

- COLONEL

You're slow. I have two minutes to, and I set mine exactly, by the tower.

- MINISTER

No, you are mistaken. Mine is as faithful as a little portable sun.

- COLONEL

Let's not argue. In a moment we'll hear the clock strike.

- MINISTER

Come, let's go. I'm hungry. There are musical instruments tuning up in my stomach. . . . (*The clock strikes*).

- COLONEL

There. Hear it? Who was right?

- MINISTER

I shall allow that, in the given instance—
(*There is the sound of a distant explosion of tremendous force*).

- MINISTER

Good heavens!

- COLONEL

Just like a munitions dump blowing up. Wow!

- MINISTER

What happened? What happened?

- COLONEL

The mountain! Look at the mountain! My God!

- MINISTER

I can't see anything, only clouds of dust. . . .

- COLONEL

No, you can see now—the summit is gone!

- MINISTER

It cannot be!

(*Hump and Lump come running in*)

20

- **LUMP**

Are you all right, Your Excellency? Some kind of terrible explosion! There's panic in the streets. Oh, look. . . .

- **MINISTER**

Out! Get out of here! Don't you dare look out the window! It's a military secret! I. . . . I don't . . . . (*Faints*).
(*Enter, running, another Official, Bump, and the Ministry Janitor Dump with a mace*)

- **COLONEL**

The Minister is unwell. Help me make him more comfortable. Get some water, and a towel. . . .

- **BUMP**

An assassination attempt! The Minister is wounded!

- **COLONEL**

Wounded nothing! Instead take a look at the mountain, the mountain, the mountain! (*Three people run in*).

- **LUMP**

It can't be! It's an optical illusion!

(*The phone rings hopelessly*).

- **DUMP**

Woe, woe. . . . The time has come of great calamities and many upheavals. . . . Woe!

- **LUMP**

And on my birthday too.

- **BUMP**

What mountain? Where is the mountain? A kingdom for a pair of glasses!

- **COLONEL**

Gently. . . . Use the towel. . . . Come on, you're only getting his uniform wet. . . . Dab the forehead! His poor, big forehead. . . . Oh, gentlemen, what a disaster!

21

(Stump comes in).

- **STUMP**

All fire brigades are on their way. The police are taking measures. The army engineers have received their orders—What happened, why is he lying down?

- **BUMP**

The explosion blew out the windows, and he was killed by flying glass.

- **STUMP**

And I'm telling you it's an earthquake. Run!

(The officials go out).

- **COLONEL**

Gentlemen, stop this disgusting confusion. He seems to be coming to.

- **MINISTER**

I'm cold. What are these wet rags doing here? Leave me alone, I want to get up. And get out of here, all of you. How dare you come piling into my office? Out! Out! . . . . *(The room empties).* Colonel!

- **COLONEL**

Come sit over here. Relax.

- **MINISTER**

Don't you understand what has happened, you idiot? Either this is some kind of horrible cosmic coincidence, or else *he* has done this!

- **COLONEL**

Relax. Everything will be cleared up in a moment.

- **MINISTER**

In the first place, stop patting my belly. And tell them to do something about that uproar outside. I have to think in peace for a moment, think in peace! Because if it's he. . . . Ah, what possibilities! Enough to drive one insane. . . . Where is he? Call him in! Don't tell me he's gone? . . . .

- COLONEL

I implore you to get a hold of yourself. The city is in a panic, and it's impossible to stop the noise. I bet it was a volcanic eruption.

- MINISTER

I want this Silvio brought here this instinct . . . insect . . . instant!

- COLONEL

What Silvio?

- MINISTER

No questions! No tensing of jaw muscles! I want that invendor . . . inwinter . . .

- COLONEL

Oh, you want to see that wretched inventor again? At your orders. (*Goes out*).

- MINISTER

Must gather my thoughts. . . . gather my thoughts. . . . Rally, my poor brain! A fantastic event has occurred, and from it I must draw a fantastic conclusion. Give me strength and wisdom, O Lord, fortify and counsel me, don't deny me your salutory. . . . Damn it, whose leg is this?

- Reporter RUMP

(*crawls out from beneath the desk*) It's all right, it's all right— I took advantage of the confusion, and happened to get in here. Allow me to ask: on the basis of certain words of yours, I infer that the Ministry is somehow implicated in this national catastrophe. . . .

- MINISTER

I'm going to shoot you!

23

- **RUMP**

. . . . or in any case knows something about its cause. . . . If you consented to explain—

(*Bump and Lump run in in answer to the bell*)

- **MINISTER**

Take him out of here and lock him up somewhere! Wait. See if there aren't any more under the furniture.

(*They find another reporter, Mump*).

- **MUMP**

(*to Rump*): Shame on you! Just because you get caught, you don't have to go squealing on me.

- **RUMP**

I swear I didn't!

- **MUMP**

Never mind—I'll smash your ribs for you.

(*They are dragged out*).

- **RUMP**

(*as he is being dragged*): Mr. Minister, tell them to lock me up separately—I have a family, I have children, my wife is preg—

- **MINISTER**

Silence! I'm certain there are others hidden in here. . . . The scoundrels! Tie them up, throw them in the cellar, cut their tongues out. . . . Oh, I can't stand it! Where is that man? Why doesn't he come?

(*Enter the Colonel and Waltz. Waltz, taking his time, reads a newspaper as he walks*).

- **COLONEL**

I had a hard time finding him! The funny fellow was calmly sitting in an alcove, reading his newspaper.

24

- MINISTER

Now then, come over here. Pleased with yourself?

- WALTZ

Just a minute, let me finish the editorial. I am partial to old newspapers. The tatters of past time. There's something touching about them. Like a garrulous pauper, to whom the tavern has long since stopped listening.

- MINISTER

No, I refuse to believe it! It's impossible. Colonel, help me, tell me he's insane!

- COLONEL

I have always said so.

- MINISTER *(to the Colonel)*

I like your cheap self-assurance. *(to Waltz)*: Look out of the window and explain.

- COLONEL

I think Mr. Waltz did not even notice the explosion. Several versions are circulating in the city. . . .

- MINISTER

Colonel, I didn't ask you. I want his opinion.

- WALTZ *(folding his newspaper)*

Well, did you like my little experiment?

- MINISTER

Don't say you want me to believe that you are responsible for this? Don't tell me you want to convince me that—Colonel, leave us alone. I lose the thread in your presence. You irritate me.

- COLONEL

Men leave, deeds remain. *(Exit)*

• WALTZ

What a change in the view. A minute ago there was an elegant cone, a picturesque Fujiyama. . . . and now there's something resembling Table Mountain. I chose it not only for its grayish grace, but also because it was uninhabited—nothing but rocks, spurge and perhaps a few lizards. The lizards, however, have perished.

• MINISTER

Listen, do you realize that you are under arrest, that you will be tried for this?

• WALTZ

For this? Oho, we are making some progress. So, now you admit I can blow up a mountain?

• MINISTER

I do not admit anything. But my reason refuses to accept this. . . . this. . . . well, this cataclysm as a simple coincidence. It's possible to predict an eclipse, but not a—. No, no, natural disasters do not occur on the stroke of noon—it is contrary to mathematics, logic, and the theory of probability.

• WALTZ

And therefore you conclude that it was done by me.

• MINISTER

If you buried some dynamite, and your henchmen set off the explosion, you will get hard labor—that's my only conclusion. Colonel! (*Rings*). Colonel! (*The Colonel comes in*). Has a report of some kind been received yet?

• COLONEL

Here it is.

• MINISTER

Give it to me. . . . Now, then. . . . "The upper half has been blown cleanly off the mountain known in the vernacular as"— what idiotic verbosity—"The part sliced of is, or was, a pyramid having an elevation of 610 meters and a base of 1415 meters in

26

diameter. A crater more than 200 meters in depth has been formed. The exploded part has been transformed into fine dust, which has either settled on the lower flanks of the decapitated mountain, or hangs like haze above the surrounding plain. Windows have been shattered. . . . no human victims. . . . great agitation in the city. . . . many have left their dwellings, fearing subterranean shocks. . . ." How nice.

• WALTZ

As I have already told you, I am a dunce in technical matters, but I think you take advantage of my ignorance when you say that I or my partners have secretly performed a highly complex mine-laying operation. Besides, I refuse to believe that you, a military expert, really think it was dynamite.

• MINISTER

Listen, Colonel, you question this person. I cannot talk to him. He keeps deliberately confusing me.

• COLONEL

At your service. So then, Mr. Waltz, you affirm that you have no connection with this business?

• MINISTER

On the contrary, on the contrary! You're going at it from the wrong end. It's the other way around—he says that—

• COLONEL

Ah! So then, Mr. Waltz, you acknowledge that you had a hand in this matter?

• MINISTER

No, this is unbearable! Your approach is all wrong. The man affirms he produced this explosion by means of his machine.

• WALTZ

Oh, infants, infants. . . . When will you begin to grow up?

27

- **COLONEL**

So then, Mr. Waltz. . . . Well, what else shall I question him about?

- **MINISTER**

Mr. Waltz, listen. I am an old man. I have seen death on the battlefield. I have witnessed many events. I do not conceal from you: what has just happened has filled me with horror, and I am overwhelmed by the most fantastic thoughts.

- **WALTZ**

And you, Colonel—did you find your cigarette case?

- **COLONEL**

None of your business. And anyway, I shall venture a little proposal. You, your Excellency, are exhausted. You will take a rest and have some lunch, while I dispatch this gentleman to the lunatic asylum. Then we shall convene a learned committee, which will instantly ascertain the real geological cause of the cataclysm.

- **MINISTER** (*to Waltz*)

Excuse him. He is indeed but an infant, and not a very bright one at that. I appeal to you now as an old man, burdened with sorrow and forebodings. I want to know the truth, no matter what that truth may be. Do not keep it from me—do not deceive an old man!

- **WALTZ**

I told you the truth half an hour before the experiment. Now you have had proof that I was not lying. Your secretary is right—relax and think it all over carefully. I assure you that, despite the apparent cruelty of my weapon, I am a humane man, much more humane than you can even imagine. You say that you have endured many things in your lifetime. Allow me to say that *my* life has consisted of such material privations, of such mental torments that now, when everything is about to change, I still feel behind my back the raw cold of the past as, after a

28

stormy night, one still feels an ominous chill in the morning shadows of the glistening garden. I feel sorry for you, I sympathize with the stabbing pain that every man experiences when his habitual world, the familiar order of life, crumbles around him. However, I must carry out my plan.

- MINISTER

What is he saying. . . . Good God, what is he saying. . . .

- COLONEL

You know my opinion. The madman is taking advantage of an understandable agitation provoked in you by a disastrous prank of nature. I can imagine what's going on in the city. The streets will be jammed, and I shall probably miss my sweet rendez-vous.

- MINISTER

Listen to me. . . . I am an old man. . . . I have. . . .

(*Trance, a reporter, comes out of a closet. He may be played by a woman*).

- TRANCE

I can't endure this rigmarole any longer. Yes, yes, Mr. Minister, I admit that my entrance is not quite proper, but I do not need to remind you how many secret assignments I have performed for you in the newspaper field, and how tightly I am able to keep my red tongue behind my white teeth. Mr. Waltz, dear colleague, my name is Trance. Your hand!

- COLONEL

What impudence! Shall I throw him out?

- MINISTER

I don't care. Let him remain. . . . I mean—her. My mind is staggering. At the moment I welcome any advisor.

- WALTZ

Here's my hand. Only why did you call me your colleague? I have never written for the newspapers, and I have burned the poems I wrote in my youth.

29

- **TRANCE**

Oh, I used that term in a deeper sense. In you I perceive a kindred soul, full of energy, resourcefulness, the fire of adventure. I have no doubt that some time later, in a moment of leisure, you will explain to me how you guessed when exactly it would occur—this interesting phenomenon, which has altered so much our celebrated vista. For the time being, though, I am of course ready to believe that you invented and used a machine. Mr. Minister, my intuition tells me this man is not a lunatic.

- **MINISTER** (*to the Colonel*)

See? I am not the only one who thinks so.

- **COLONEL**

Until he is examined by a doctor I shall abide by my original opinion.

- **TRANCE**

Fine. Let everybody keep his opinion, and let us play.

- **WALTZ**

Yes, let us play. The Colonel takes me for a paranoiac, the Minister thinks I am a demon, and you hint I am a quack. I, of course, shall keep to my own opinion.

- **MINISTER**

Well, Trance, you see, what a strange situation we are in—

- **TRANCE**

My dear Mr. Minister, nothing strange ever happens in life. You are faced with a certain fact, and you must either accept that fact or admit your mental incompetence. I propose the following: let some further experiments be made. You can arrange that, can't you, Mr. Waltz?

- **WALTZ**

Yes, I shall have to. Apparently the ground has not been adequately prepared yet.

30

- **TRANCE**

Oh, I'd say you deal with the ground in a rather cavalier way, (To the Minister): Well, what do you say to my proposal?

- **MINISTER**

I'm thinking, I'm thinking.

- **TRANCE**

Better don't think—it might make matters worse.

- **COLONEL** (*to Waltz*)

No, please move over. I want to be next to my chief.

- **WALTZ**

I am more comfortable right here.

- **COLONEL**

And I'm telling you—

- **TRANCE**

Gentlemen, don't squabble. (*To the Minister*): Well, have you done thinking?

- **MINISTER**

My responsibility is colossal, my power of decision, nil. . . . The possibility of finding myself in a ridiculous position is intolerable. . . . The President will set loose public opinion upon me. . . . It will tear me apart. . . .

- **WALTZ**

That is now quite irrelevant. I am asking you if you want further demonstrations, or if the one you saw today is sufficient. That's the question.

- **COLONEL**

I forbid you to speak to my Minister in this way!

- **TRANCE**

Gentlemen, we are all a little excited, and therefore a certain

31

sharpness of speech is pardonable. (*To the Minister*): Do finish thinking, please.

• MINISTER

And no one to turn to for advice. . . . The fear of divulging this secret. . . . The fear. . . .

• TRANCE

It's so simple—appoint a commission of trustworthy people, and let's play. Colonel, leave that chair alone. This is really no time for trifles.

• COLONEL

I don't want him to sit there.

• TRANCE

Forget it, forget it. Well, Mr. Minister?

• MINISTER

I don't know. . . . I am unable. . . .

• WALTZ

He's taking too long to think. It's revolting. Let's go, Trance, I can use you.

• MINISTER

Oh, so you are surprised at my state of mind? Then allow me to inform you that I understand certain things that you do not. I am a man of vision, and I picture so clearly all that our country can extract. . . . And on the other hand. . . . All right, I'll risk it! Further tests shall be made.

• TRANCE

These are historic words. I am happy and proud that I am present to hear them. Yes, I think the tests must be made, and that our inventor will meet the challenge brilliantly. Isn't that so, Waltz? Of course, you will be given time for preparation.

• WALTZ

All I need is to be able to give orders by radio half an hour before the test.

- TRANCE

Of course, of course. . . . Well, I'm very glad to have resolved this matter.

- MINISTER

If, however, nothing comes of these tests, two things will have been lost irrevocably: my reputation and this gentleman's life.

- WALTZ

I shall only observe that logic does not tolerate mixing apprehension and menace the way you do.

- COLONEL

We shall see, we shall see! One wonders what countenance you will have when the experts ascertain why and how precisely the mountain disintegrated. It used to be so beautiful! Many a time at nightfall, its violet cone, against the background of a golden sky, would evoke in me and in my sweetheart of the moment marvelous thoughts about man's insignificance, about the grandeur and tranquility of Mother Nature. I used to shed tears. . . .

- TRANCE

Mr. Waltz has tripped Mother Nature and made her fall flat on her face. (*To the Minister*): So what next?

- MINISTER

Next. . . . Well, we shall make three or four tests. Dependable people will have to be gathered, and the locations selected.

- WALTZ

And all this as quickly as possible.

- MINISTER

And all this as quickly as possible. . . . Just a minute, though, why all the hurry? Or do you intend to offer your invention to somebody else?

- WALTZ

33

My impatience should not surprise you: the check has been written out. There is no sense in delaying the payment.

- MINISTER

My dear fellow, please don't speak in conundrums. Speak so that people can understand you—people who are moreover weary and jumpy.

- TRANCE

Easy, easy. We have now settled everything and may go home.

- COLONEL

We don't even know the address of the hospital from which he escaped.

- WALTZ

I am staying at a hotel. Here is the address. (*Jots it down*).

- TRANCE

Yes, yes, we believe you, as my former husbands used to say. All right, then. Don't put it off, Mr. Minister. Assemble the commission and let's start the tests, the earlier the better. And you, Waltz, don't get impatient. I'll see to it that there is no delay.

- WALTZ

I'll wait three days—no more.

- TRANCE

Say, four days. You know, these are all venerable old fellows, and it's not easy to get them going.

- MINISTER

However, there is one condition I must make, gentlemen. Everything that has been said here is a top military secret—not a word must reach the public.

- TRANCE

Oh, all right. My paper will keep mum. At least until just a few hours before other papers publish the glad news.

- **MINISTER**

How nastily you put it . . . . What a rascal you are. . . . Listen, Colonel—what about those two other reporters we caught in here?

- **COLONEL**

Locked up. But I venture to observe that it's impossible to hold them for long. It's against the law. There will be questions in Parliament, and you know what a bother that is.

- **MINISTER**

Never mind. I'll talk to the President. We'll force the scoundrels to keep quiet.

- **WALTZ** (*looking at a large book on a table*)

Funny thing—this atlas, this particular copy belonged to me once, in school. With the same blot on Corsica.

- **COLONEL**

Only that's not Corsica but Sardinia.

- **WALTZ**

Then the inscription is wrong.

- **COLONEL**

Your Excellency, make him stop teasing me.

- **TRANCE**

Quiet, quiet. Waltz, I think now everything has been settled and we can withdraw.

- **MINISTER**

Only remember: secrecy! I implore you! Have your paper print a story about an earthquake, a volcano, anything you like— but not a peep, gentlemen, not a peep. . . .

(*General Gump and his daughter Annabella come in*).

- **GENERAL GUMP**

We come in unannounced—Does it matter? We're at home here. Har, har, har (*This is how he laughs*).

35

- **MINISTER**

I can't see you right now, General. I'm busy.

- **GUMP**

Ah, there he is, the culprit, the cause of all the commotion, har har, har. Well, dear Mr. Minister, my protégé is not so crazy after all, eh?

- **MINISTER**

For heaven's sake, General, don't boom it out for the whole Ministry to hear, we'll have a talk later. . . .

- **GUMP**

What an explosion! Magnificent in its simplicity and power! Sliced off the top like a knife. And you tell me he's a lunatic. Some lunatic!

- **MINISTER**

What makes you think he did it? We don't know anything yet.

- **GUMP**

Who else? Of course it was he. Atta boy! (*To Waltz*): You must show me your machine.

- **WALTZ**

The hell I must.

- **GUMP**

And proud as a rooster too! No, this is marvelous. This is even artistic. I saw right away there was something special about him. (*To the Minister*): By the way, tell me—you didn't forget to do something about the widow? I forgot to add that—

- **MINISTER**

Later, later. . . . Gentlemen, excuse me. I must leave. I'm worn out. Have pity on me!

- **ANNABELLA** (*going up to Waltz*)

So it was really you who blew up the mountain?

36

- **WALTZ**

It was done on my orders.

- **ANNABELLA**

And did you know who lived there once upon a time?

- **WALTZ**

No. Who?

- **ANNABELLA**

An old enchanter and a snow-white gazelle.

Curtain

Act Two

Seated at a long table: The Minister of War, the Colonel, and eleven old generals, Bump, Dump, Gump, Hump, Lump, Mump, Rump, Stump, Tump, Ump, Zump. (The last three are represented by dummies but differ little from the rest).

• MINISTER

Well, I think everyone is present.

• MUMP

Where is Bump? Bump is not here yet.

• LUMP

What do you mean? There he is.

• GUMP

Har, Har, Har.

• RUMP (to Bump)

What's the matter, General—Why don't people notice you? After all, you arn't so small.

• MUMP

Sorry, I somehow overlooked you. Yes, we are all here.

• MINISTER

Good, let us commence.

• GUMP (to Bump)

To go unnoticed means wealth.

38

- **STUMP** (*to Mump*)

You probably didn't notice him because he's nearsighted. (*They all laugh*).

- **BUMP**

Yes, that is my misfortune.

- **MUMP**

No, I just did not see the general enter. By the way, Gentlemen, you know something? There are thirteen of us!

- **MINISTER**

We cannot ask the inventor in before the end of the meeting, and the President won't get here before five. It's unpleasant that we are thirteen. . . .

- **GUMP**

Yes, but one of us has no *voice*, har-har!

      (*The implied* Hump *vigorously uses his rattle*).

- **COLONEL**

I can withdraw if someone will agree to act as secretary in my place.

- **MINISTER**

No, why should you? Only it's unpleasant. . . .

- **COLONEL**

I'll be glad to go. . . .

- **MINISTER**

Oh, why do you take offense at every word? It really is tiresome!

- **RUMP**

Couldn't we invite that nice mining engineer of mine—you know, the blond one with the whiskers?—he's in the know, anyway.

- **LUMP**

It would be against the rules. I object.

39

•   RUMP (*wistfully*)

You liked him so much when I introduced him to you at the
Amethyst Club.

•   MINISTER

Tell me, please, what is that trunk doing in the corner?

•   COLONEL

Oh, that's from the archives. It contains maps and charts.

•   STUMP

You mean: chaps and marts?

•   GUMP

Har, har, har.

•   COLONEL

No, I said "caps." I mean "maps." I had them brought because
I thought they might be useful. If you wish, I can have them
removed.

•   MINISTER

Please open the trunk, my dear Colonel. (*Trance issues from the
trunk*).

•   MINISTER

I thought so.

•   TRANCE

Where do you wish me to sit?

•   MUMP

There are still thirteen of us! One, two, three. . . (*He counts*).
That's curious.

•   BUMP

You've forgotten me again.

•   MUMP

Yes, that's right.

40

- MINISTER

Fine. Let us begin now. Only remember, Trance—you have no vote. Sit there and keep quiet.

- LUMP

I object. There must be no outsiders.

- GUMP

Oh, come on, General. He's merely a figment of the imagination. A trance, a daze, a dream. There are no more of us than before.

- LUMP

In that case I withdraw my objection.

- MINISTER

Gentlemen! We shall now hear a report concerning the three tests conducted by . . . conducted (*looks up the name*) by Salvator Waltz. This seems a mere formality, since in one way or another you all know the results already; at the same time, however, we need this formality, as a basis for our debate. I shall ask you to concentrate. We must take this very day an important decision whose full significance cannot be . . . minimized. Gentlemen, I shall ask you to listen carefully—and if possible, General Dump, not to doodle during the reading of the report.

- DUMP

It helps me to listen. It really does.

- MINISTER

No, you always draw such complicated things. And look, you even add shading. It's revolting.

- RUMP (*to Dump*)

Let's see. Well, if that's supposed to be a motor car, it doesn't look much like one.

- MINISTER

In any case, please stop it. The meeting is in session, and we

41

shall now hear the report. Who has the report? I think you do, Rump?

- **RUMP**

No, General Mump has it.

- **MUMP**

I beg your pardon, I do *not* have it. Stop tattling.

- **MINISTER**

Who has it then, Gentlemen? Wasn't it you who wrote it, Rump?

- **RUMP**

We compiled it jointly, and then General Lump passed it on.

- **MINISTER**

To whom did you give it, Lump?

- **LUMP**

I'd like to know why General Rump puts the blame on others. I never saw that report. I happen to know, though, that General Dump has it.

- **DUMP**

What report?

- **BUMP**

If you will allow me. Ump copied out the report, and Tump checked it over.

- **MINISTER** (*To Ump and Tump*)

That means you have it? (*They, naturally do not respond*).

- **GUMP**

Gone with the wind. Har, har, har.

- **MINISTER**

All right, we'll do it differently. I shall ask whoever has the report to raise his hand. No one raises his hand? Splendid. This means the report has been lost, if it ever was written.

42

•   LUMP

In this connection I move that the report be prepared once again and that the meeting be adjourned to a later date.

•   MINISTER

You don't know what you are saying. It's disgusting! How mean of you to say that! Listen, Colonel, can you explain what happened to the report?

•   COLONEL

I had absolutely nothing to do with it.

•   MINISTER

And I'm telling you that you had. And you know why? From the very beginning you took the position that none of this was any business of yours, that . . . that we . . . are engaged in nonsense, and that . . . this inventor is simply a lunatic. You have been sulking and pouting, and now it's happened, and you can be pleased with yourself.

•   COLONEL

Your Excellency, I am bound to perform my official duty, and I fulfil it to the best of my humble ability. But my personal opinion I cannot change.

•   MUMP

I second General Lump's motion. My dear Minister, let us postpone this whole business. . . . Why waste our time? Let's meet next week, when we are nice and fresh—won't that be better?

•   MINISTER

Splendid. In that case I submit my resignation immediately. Who is in favor of the stated motion? Will those who are in favor stand. No one is going to stand? The motion is defeated. Now *I* shall introduce a motion. I shall ask you, General Lump, to make the report orally.

•   LUMP

Why me? We all worked on it together.

- **MINISTER**

Splendid. The meeting is closed, and I shall ask the President immediately to find a successor to my office.

- **LUMP**

Wait a minute, wait a minute. . . . You didn't ask General Hump, you know—why don't you ask him?
(*Hump rises. He is dumb, but endeavors to say something in sign language*).

- **MINISTER**

Unfortunately I do not understand the language of mutes. You ought to see a doctor if you are mute. It's revolting! There exists a specialist who can teach you—at least to make some kind of a mooing sound.

- **VOICES:**

Tell us about it! Oh, please! We beg you! It's so interesting!

- **MINISTER**

Silence! The only way out of this absurd situation—

- **TRANCE**

May I put in a word?

- **LUMP**

It is illegal.

- **TRANCE**

I'll put in a word, like a coin in a slot, and everything will start moving at once—you'll see!

- **MINISTER**

Go ahead. I don't care.

- **TRANCE**

I shall make the report. After all, I am just as well informed as any of you, if not better. Agreed?

44

- **LUMP**

I withdraw my objection.

- **MINISTER**

Well, why not?—Gentlemen, I think we shall ask Trance—After all, it's only a formality, we all know the contents of the report, only he will give it a concise and exact form. I don't think we need vote. Is everyone agreed? Trance, you have the floor.

- **TRANCE**

I shall be brief. On the day before yesterday Salvator Waltz was asked to fulfill three assignments: to blow up a rocky island situated one hundred miles from a desert shore—you will excuse me, Gentlemen, I deliberately do not mention any place names, so as not to overburden my report—and anyway you know where those places are.

- **VOICES:**

Yes, yes, it's unnecessary. . . . These are details. . . . Small print. . . .

- **TRANCE**

The other places you had selected were: a spot in the middle of an impenetrable swamp; and another, in a sandy desert. The exact location of these spots was communicated to Waltz at precisely six A.M., and he immediately withdrew saying he was going to get in touch with his partner. Observation showed that he really did give orders by radio, in code so as not to alarm chance listeners. Aircraft were sent out in advance to observe the results from a safe distance. At half past six—that is, exactly half an hour later—the island was totally destroyed. At exactly seven A.M. an explosion took place in the swamp, and another half hour later boom went the desert.

- **VOICES:**

Wonderful! This is wonderful! Just think! This is absolutely sensational!

45

- **TRANCE**

There was, however, a fair share of curious incidents, and rather regrettable ones at that. Some idiot in a private plane, attempting a record flight, somehow got among the aircraft observing the destruction of the island. The explosion in the swamp for some reason caused an immediate drying up of the river that serves the main town of that remote province. Finally, and this is most vexing, several hours after the explosion a famous explorer—whose name you will learn from the newspapers—came on the colossal crater left in the middle of the desert, and, it seems, found it highly interesting.

- **VOICES:**

Well, that really *is* interesting. Only natural to become interested! What a discovery!

- **MINISTER** (*to Trance*)

Am I to assume from your words that news of these three. . . .

events. . . . will spread through the city before the end of the day?

- **TRANCE**

I'm afraid it's unavoidable, and it will be necessary to think up something a bit more convincing than the earthquake story launched in connection with the decapitated mountain. All the more since the public did not believe this story.

- **MINISTER**

Yes, yes—we'll think up something. I don't know. . . . My head is spinning. . . . Later—we'll discuss it later.

- **BUMP**

I have a question: Should we not seek the causes of the interesting phenomena, so vividly described by the speaker—should we not, I say, seek their causes in the overheating of the ground resulting from this year's unusually warm spring?

- **MINISTER**

I do not understand what you are talking about.

46

- **TRANCE**

It's all right—it's nothing, the General is only airing some learned hypotheses. Allow me to finish, though. Gentlemen, all of you took part in the selection of the sites, and all of you heard the report. Thus you have been able to convince yourselves that, *primo*, Salvator Waltz has fulfilled his assignments and, *secundo*, fulfilled it in such a period of time and under such conditions as to exclude all possibility of mass collaboration.

- **VOICES:**

Yes! Of course! Obvious! Goes without saying!

- **TRANCE**

Furthermore, I should like to call your attention to the following. Not knowing where Waltz's device is located, we of course cannot know if Waltz is correct in his assertion that this Tele-mort, as he lovingly dubs it, is effective at *any* distance. Nevertheless the fact that the first of the spots you selected is four hundred miles distant from the second proves that range and military effectiveness of the device exceed the boldest dreams!

- **MINISTER**

Are you through, Trance?

- **TRANCE**

In a general way—that is all.

- **MINISTER**

Does anyone wish to comment on the matter? No one? I see a smile on your face, Colonel.

- **COLONEL**

You know my opinion, Sir. Until the mental health of this Waltz has been checked by doctors, I cannot take him seriously.

- **LUMP**

Hear, hear! I propose that everything be postponed until there has been a medical examination.

47

- **MUMP**

Me too! We must know first of all with whom we are dealing.

- **MINISTER**

Splendid. The meeting is adjourned. I have no doubt that the President will accept my resignation this very day.

- **LUMP**

I withdraw my proposal.

- **MUMP**

I agree.

- **LUMP**

Reopen the meeting.

- **VOICES:**

Please! please!

- **MINISTER**

I warn you that if there is so much as another hint at the inventor's being insane, I shall put on my cap and leave. The meeting is in session. I take the floor. So, Gentlemen, the tests have been made and have given results that are positive to say the least. (*To Dump*): You would like to say something, General?

- **DUMP**

No, no—I'm looking for my little pencil.

- **MINISTER**

Positive, to say the least. The inventor has proved that his machine possesses fantastic power. In other words, a government disposing of such a weapon would gain a unique position in the world. At the present moment, in view of the intrigues of our belligerent neighbors, such a position is exceedingly tempting. We would be able, without mobilizing a single soldier, to impose our will on the entire world. This is the single deduction that we are duty-bound to draw; therefore, right now, without delay, I want to ask you a question, Gentlemen, to which I demand a considered and definite answer: what, practically speaking, should be our next move? Bump, I shall ask your opinion.

- BUMP

Our next move, our considered step, must be. . . . must be. . . . it must be definite.

- MINISTER

Is that all?

- BUMP

Actually, I. . . . Yes, that's all.

- MINISTER

Sit down. You, Mump.

- MUMP

Me?

- MINISTER

Yes, yes, you. Well?

- MUMP

I didn't prepare today's assignment. One would like to study the question more closely. . . . I've been sick. . . . a mild case of sclerosis. . . .

- MINISTER

In that case you should have brought a note from your children. Not good at all! Sit down. Dump!

- DUMP

Excuse me, I did not hear the question.

- MINISTER

No wonder. I shall repeat it. What, in your opinion. . . . I think you have your hand up, Stump. No? Too bad. Sit down, Dump. Not good at all! All right, Lump.

49

To My Soul

My Soul, how fierce is your impatience,
How gladly home you would have flown,
Out of the marvelously fashioned,
But much too narrow cage of bone!

Your home I do not know, believe me!
Even the way there, is not clear,
And when you fly, how shall I follow
With so much booty taken here?

•   MINISTER

Are you in your right mind?

•   LUMP

It's the poem by Tourvalski. It was assigned for homework.

•   MINISTER

Quiet! (Hump *rattles*). Oh, curse it, I don't want to hear that thing anymore, take it away from him, somebody! (*This is done*).

•   STUMP (*hand up*)

May I? I know the answer.

•   MINISTER

Shame on you, Gentlemen. Here, the oldest and most decrepit one has it, and you don't know a damn thing. Shame! Go ahead, Stump.

•   STUMP

Our next move should be as follows: we must ask him (Indicating Trance) to put all this in writing and give us a detailed description of his telegum.

•   MINISTER

Really? Unfortunately, General, this is not the person we are discussing. You may sit down. There, Colonel, I hope you are

50

pleased with the results of your attitude. Nobody knows anything or wants to know anything, and meanwhile we are facing a problem of national importance, on whose solution depends our entire future. If you do not wish to work, Gentlemen, there is no sense in coming here. You can just as well sit on your stoops in the sunshine and suck your lips—that would be best.

(*Deathly silence*).

• MINISTER

Perhaps you will answer the question, Trance?

• TRANCE

The answer is crystal-clear.

• MINISTER

Go ahead.

• TRANCE

We must immediately buy from Sal Waltz his wonderful gadget.

• MINISTER

There. That's correct. A new boy, and yet he had the right answer while the rest of you sit around like saps. Yes, Gentlemen, we must buy it. Is everyone agreed?

• VOICES:

Buy it! Buy it! Why not? Of course we should buy it!

• GUMP

A mule bought is a fool caught. Har, har, har.

• MINISTER

The motion is passed, then. Now we have to discuss the price. What figure can we set?

• LUMP

Nine hundred.

• MUMP

Nine hundred twenty.

51

- RUMP

One thousand.

- LUMP

Two thousand. (*Pause*).

- MINISTER

So, the last figure named was—

- MUMP

Twenty-two hundred.

- LUMP

Three thousand.

- MINISTER

The last figure named—

- MUMP

Thirty-two hundred. (*Pause*).

- MINISTER

Was thirty-two hundred. . . .

- LUMP

Ten thousand.

- MUMP

Ten thousand two hundred.

- LUMP

Twenty thousand.

- STUMP

And I say one million. (*Sensation.* Ump *slides down from his chair and is propped back*).

- MINISTER

I think we'll stop at that figure.

- VOICES:

No, why? It was such fun! Let's go on!

52

- **MINISTER**

Stop the noise! One million is as high as we can go, if he begins bargaining. Our initial offer will be, say, two thousand.

- **MUMP**

Twenty-two hundred.

- **MINISTER**

Discussion of this matter is closed, General.

- **TRANCE**

And the time has come to ask in the seller.

- **MINISTER**

Colonel, please call him.

- **COLONEL**

I shall not betray what my feelings are. I am performing my duty.

- **MINISTER**

Well, you know, in this state of mind you had better not go. Stay seated, stay seated—never mind, you and I will have another chat about this, you can rest assured. . . . Miss France, I mean, Miss Trance, would you fetch him? He is waiting, if I am not mistaken, in the Hall of Mirrors. You know the way?

(*The Colonel, sulking, has walked to the window*).

- **TRANCE**

I certainly do. (*Goes out*).

- **MINISTER**

I call a five-minute recess.

- **STUMP**

Ow, ow, ow, my foot is asleep.

- **LUMP**

Now wait a minute—that's an artificial leg you have here.

53

- **STUMP**

Ah, that's what the matter is.

- **BUMP** (*to Gump*)

I say, General, why do you treat your daughter so strictly? My family tells me you don't even let her go to the theater with a girl-friend?

- **GUMP**

That's right, I don't. (*Consults his watch*). Must not be late for that funeral. Catch up with it on the way.

- **MINISTER**

Oh, if you only knew, Gentlemen, what a headache I have! Haven't slept for three nights in a row. . . .

- **MUMP** (*to Lump*)

What do you think, are we going to get something to drink?

- **LUMP**

Last time we got loaded, so now they won't give us any.

- **MUMP**

That's not true! I've never been drunk in my life.

- **COLONEL** (*at the window*)

Good heavens, what's going on in the street! People carrying signs, shouting. . . . I'll open the door to the balcony.

(*They all pour out on the balcony, except Stump, Tump, Ump, and* Hump *who is sulking or sleeping, or both*). (*Trance and Waltz come in*)

- **TRANCE**

Sit down, make yourself at home.

- **WALTZ**

The more I watch you, the better I see that you can be very useful to me.

- **TRANCE**

Always at your service.

54

- **WALTZ**

Only I want to ask you to drop that familiar, facetious manner in which you permit yourself to address me. You have never been and never will be my associate, but if you wish to run errands for me, then behave like a subordinate, and not like a tipsy conspirator.

- **TRANCE**

Everything will depend on the amount of tangible gratitude that you will agree to accord me on a monthly basis. There, you see: I use your language.

- **WALTZ**

Gratitude? That's the first time I hear that word. Gratitude: a dark ruby. Hm.

- **TRANCE**

In a minute you will see for yourself that I have put in some good work for you. The old fellows are going to make you an offer not devoid of interest, only don't be in a hurry to accept. Without me they would never have arrived at a decision.

- **WALTZ**

That's right, keep alert, it will come in handy. To-morrow, of course, I shall have all the servants I wish. You turned up ahead of time, luckily for you, and I am engaging you as a factotum.

- **TRANCE**

Bear in mind that I am not yet acquainted with the exact rules of your game, and I follow them by intuition.

- **WALTZ**

My game has only one rule—love of mankind.

- **TRANCE**

Not asking much, are you? This is incongruous, though: you deprive me of the humble rights of a Leporello, while yourself you aspire to be Don Juan to the whole world.

55

- **WALTZ**

I don't think for a minute that you are capable of understanding my intentions. I am tired of waiting. Call them in—it's time to have done with the old world.

- **TRANCE**

Listen, darling, I must admit I'm terribly curious. . . . We understand each other perfectly well, so there's no need to keep up formalities. Tell me, how do you do it?

- **WALTZ**

Do what?

- **TRANCE**

Those explosions, of course.

- **WALTZ**

I don't understand. You would like to know how my machine works?

- **TRANCE**

Cut it out, Waltz. Forget about the machine—you can tell it to them, not to me. It's not even the explosion itself that interests me—anybody can lay a mine—what interests me is how you guess the spot beforehand.

- **WALTZ**

What need have I to guess?

- **TRANCE**

Yes, I used the wrong word. Of course you cannot know in advance what islands and deserts they will indicate to you. . . . but you can, like a conjuror, force a card into one's hand. . . . What I'm saying is that, if you have people helping you here, then it's not so difficult to suggest to our experts what spot they ought to choose for, an explosion—and, there, everything is ready and waiting to blow up. That's how it works, eh?

- **WALTZ**

An idiotic procedure.

• TRANCE

Oh, I know, I know—actually it is all much more complicated
and subtle. You're a remarkable gambler. I was just saying this
by way of an example. . . . You know, I try to catch your
obscure words on the wing so as to guess your intentions. . . .
It was I, for example, who suggested the island—I thought you
had alluded to it in passing. Didn't you?

• WALTZ

Nonsense.

• TRANCE

Waltz, sweet boy, come, don't be so shy, come, I know there's
a big secret there, come, undo just one little button and show it
to me. I promise I'll be yours until the day I die.

• WALTZ

Down, dog.

• TRANCE

All right, but when will you tell me—soon? Tomorrow?

• WALTZ

Call those people, please.

• TRANCE

Tough nut to crack. (*She carries out the order. They all come
back from the balcony, gaily comparing notes*).

• RUMP

A most picturesque manifestation. Those schoolboys were really
cute!

• STUMP

Tell me, did you read that last sign?

• MUMP

Which one? "We want the truth?" Was that the one?

57

- **STUMP**

No, no. The rhymed one was "They blow up the desert to-day, to-morrow us they will slay." What's the meaning of it? What's the occasion? Is it election time?

- **MINISTER**

All this is most deplorable. It was a military secret!

- **DUMP**

The one I liked best was: "Blast the Blasters!" Simple and forceful.

- **LUMP** (*Interpreting Hump's sign language*)

Hump says there hasn't been such excitement since the time the king was assassinated.

- **BUMP**

My misfortune is that glaucoma defies glasses. . . .

- **MINISTER**

How tiresome. How aggravating! I'll have to recruit some scientists, and let them think up an explanation of some sort. . . . (*Noticing Waltz*). Ah, here he is. How do you do? Please sit down. Gentlemen, take your seats. I recall the meeting to order. Colonel!

- **COLONEL**

Yes, Sir?

- **MINISTER**

You have that memo, haven't you—No, not that—the scrap with his name. . . . Thank you. Now then. . . . Mr. Salvator Waltz, the committee under my chairmanship has thoroughly examined and discussed the results of your experiments. After a thorough examination we have reached the conclusion that your invention presents a certain interest for us. In other words, we would be inclined to enter upon negotiations with you in regard to the possibility of acquiring your apparatus—

- **GUMP**

—apparatus to evaporate us. Har, har, har!

- **MINISTER**

That jingle was out of place. Stop the laughter! Rump, stop
whispering to your neighbor. Gump, stop looking at your watch.
Who's giggling there? What kind of behavior is this? I continue. . . . say, where do you think you are going, general?

- **GUMP**

Funeral! Almost forgot Perrault's funeral. Catch up with it on
the brink of the grave—Har . . . (*goes out guffawing*).

- **MINISTER**

We are inclined to acquire, or, more exactly, to purchase, your
invention. It is true that at this moment our treasury is not rich,
but I nevertheless flatter myself with the hope that the sum we
can offer you will seem to you a more than fair reward. We
offer you two thousand crowns.

- **WALTZ**

I didn't quite understand. What do you want to pay me for? For
the tests I conducted?

- **MINISTER**

It's no wonder you didn't hear me—the surroundings are impossible. Gentlemen, I refuse to speak unless you stop whispering
and giggling. What's the matter? What do you have under the
table there? Dump! Mump!

- **DUMP**

We aren't doing anything, word of honor.

- **MINISTER**

Then don't fidget. (*To Waltz*): I am not speaking about those
tests, but suggesting that you sell us your machine for two
thousand. Naturally, the transaction will take place only after
you let us see the thing.

- **WALTZ**

What a delightful misunderstanding! You want to buy my
machine? For two thousand?

- **MINISTER**

59

Yes. I suppose, however, that we might, as a very special exception, increase the figure to three.

- WALTZ

Trance, they want to buy my Telemort! Trance, did you hear that?

- TRANCE

Haggle, haggle! You hold the trump card.

- MINISTER

I should think that three thousand, let us even say four, is a sum considerably in excess of your expences. As you see, we are ready to meet you half way.

- WALTZ

You are positively rushing to the meeting place. But alas, I am obliged to interrupt your impetus. You are laboring under a ridiculous misconception. My machine is not for sale.

(*Short pause*).

- MINISTER

What do you mean, not for sale?

- WALTZ

Of course not! What a crazy idea!

- TRANCE

Take a little hint from a big operator: don't pour it on too thick, Waltz.

- MINISTER

My dear fellow, I have not finished—I am perfectly willing to offer you a higher price, if the present one seems inadequate to you, though I, personally. . . . Even though I personally. . . . In short, will you accept ten thousand?

- WALTZ

Forget it. It's time to get down to business.

60

- MINISTER

But that's just what I am doing! Well, let's say twenty, let's say fifty. . . . Gentlemen, help me—why do you sit there like dummies?

- STUMP

One million.

- MINISTER

All right, a million. This. . . . this is a fantastic price, and it will be necessary to introduce new taxes, but no matter, I'll go along with it: one million.

- TRANCE

Waltz, that's a lot of money.

- WALTZ

And I am telling you that I do not intend selling anything to anyone.

- TRANCE

What nerves of iron!

- MINISTER

Am I correct in assuming that you will not sell your machine even for a million?

- WALTZ

Correct.

- MINISTER

And that you will not name your own price? Bear in mind that we are prepared to consider any price you name.

- TRANCE

Now, Waltz. This is the moment.

- WALTZ

That's enough. I didn't come here for this. Gentlemen, I have no merchandise to offer you.

- MINISTER

Is that your last word?

- WALTZ

On this subject, yes. Now we shall discuss something quite different.

- MINISTER

You are right. You are quite right, Mr. Inventor. We shall indeed discuss something else now. You found fit to shout "That's enough." Now, I, too, would like to say "That's enough!" Since you do not wish to let us have your gadget, I shall immediately arrest you, and you'll remain in prison until you argee to the transaction. That's enough, Mr. Inventor! You will see. . . . You. . . . I'll force you. . . . Or you'll rot in a stone cell. . . . and everyone will support me in this, since the object you possess is much too dangerous to remain in private hands. Enough of your scheming! What do you think we are, fools? You think tomorrow you will go bargain with our neighbors? Like fun you will! Either you agree immediately, or I call the guards.

- WALTZ

I think that's the second time you threaten to deprive me of my liberty—as if it were possible to deprive me of liberty!

- MINISTER

You are under arrest! You no longer exist! Colonel, take the necessary action. . . .

- COLONEL

Oh, yes, with pleasure. It's high time!

- VOICES:

Yes, it's high time! Hack him to pieces! Defenestrate him! Draw and quarter him!

- TRANCE

One moment, General. Let's not lose our heads—such as they

62

are, they're still heads, and one mustn't lose 'em, they have some sentimental value. Gentlemen, and you, darling, I am certain that these methods of persuasion are excessive. Let Waltz consider your proposal—that is, one million before delivery, and one million after—and I am convinced that everything will end peacefully. Isn't that so, pet?

- WALTZ

I am tired of repeating that my machine is not for sale.

- MINISTER

Quick, Colonel! Take him away, tie him up, drag him off! To jail! To the fortress! To the dungeon!

- WALTZ

And in seven hours, that is, exactly at midnight, there will take place a curious and highly instructive event.

- MINISTER

Colonel, wait. (*To Waltz*): What.... event?

- WALTZ

I foresaw an attempt to intimidate me and have made an arrangement with my anonymous partner: Unless he hears from me by midnight, he is to blow up one of your most flourishing cities. I shall not say which one—let it be a surprise.

- MINISTER

It can't be.... Fate cannot be so cruel to me....

- WALTZ

And that is not all. If, by five minutes after the explosion, there is no signal from me, then another town will go up in smoke. And this will be repeated every five minutes, until my liberation—or resurrection.

- MINISTER

He's right. . . . He's right. . . . He has thought of every-

63

thing! . . . . Can't you make some suggestion, you wretches?

- **LUMP**

To jail, to jail!

- **COLONEL**

Before I commit hara-kiri, I once again raise my voice and firmly repeat: send this man to the insane asylum.

- **WALTZ**

I don't think there is any point in waiting for the President of the Republic to join us. Let us begin. Squeeze together, please, I'm uncomfortable here. Now be so kind as to hear me out.

- **MINISTER** (*kneeling on the floor*)

Mr. Inventor, I am a very old, very respectable man—and you see me on my knees before you. Sell us your little machine!

- **VOICES:**

What is the Minister doing? What is this? Get up, Your Excellency. . . . He is not worth it. . . . This is unheard of. . . .

- **COLONEL**

I cannot see this humiliation.

- **MINISTER**

I implore you. . . . No, let me be—I shall force him to heed me. . . . Have pity. . . . Any price you want. . . . I implore you. . . .

- **WALTZ**

Take him away, please. He has slobbered all over my pants.

- **MINISTER** (*on his feet*)

Give me some sharp object! Colonel, let us die together. My

friend, my dearest Colonel. . . . What a dreadful situation. . . .
Quick, a dagger! (*To Rump*): What's this?

· RUMP

A letter-opener. I don't know—Hump gave it to me.

· VOICES:

Oh, show us how it's done. . . . Try using it. . . . It'll work
fine. . . . Please. . . .

· COLONEL

Traitors!

· TRANCE

Quiet, gentlemen, quiet. I think a speech is about to be made.
You, Mr. Minister, will have to share my chair—I can give you
the edge—since your own chair is now taken. I am very much
interested to hear what he will say.

· WALTZ

Attention, Gentlemen! I now declare
The start of a new life. Be welcome, Life!

· LUMP

Should we stand up?

· MUMP

Should we?

· WALTZ

You may listen in a sitting position, or even supine, if you wish.
(*General laughter*). What a humorous mood you are in, gentlemen!

· MINISTER

It's the excitement that makes them like that. Their nerves have
given way. . . . I myself. . . . But proceed, proceed.

65

- **WALTZ**

> Gone is the old and musty world. Now Spring
> Through Time's wide-open window rushes in,
> And I who stand before you, am today—
> Though yesterday a pauper and a dreamer—
> Master omnipotent of every land.
> I have been called to renovate the world
> And roll away toward the nearest exit
> The ashcans of the Past. Oh, blissful toil!

May I ask you—sorry, I don't know your name—

- **RUMP**

This is Dump.

- **WALTZ**

May I ask you, Mr. Dump, why do you have this toy car on the table? It's strange. . . .

- **DUMP**

I'm not playing with anything—really and truly, they can confirm it.

- **WALTZ**

Then you have just hidden it under the table. I saw it perfectly well. It even seemed to me it was that same little red car with the paint scratched off on one side of the hood that I had when I was a boy. Where is it? You were rolling it to and fro on the table only a moment ago. (*Music is heard from above*).

- **DUMP**

No, no, I swear. . . .

- **VOICES:**

There is no toy here. . . . Dump isn't lying. Word of honor. . . .

- **WALTZ**

In that case I must have imagined it. Probably that accursed music overhead is also imaginary.

- **MINISTER**

Go on, go on. Waiting for your decision is unbearable.

- **WALTZ**

> Oh, blissful toil! Long have I tried to solve
> The problem of your world—that problem—bristling
> With such uncertain data, spectral numbers,
> And obstacles, and traps for a man's mind!
> Long have I tried to solve or give it up
> Till suddenly the live spark of the "X"
> Burst into flame and furnished the solution.
> Now all is clear to me. My secret engine
> Is surer than hereditary crowns,
> Popular vote, or a dictator's fury.
> Not that I wish to sop my reign in kindness:
> A threat can work much better with a child
> Than any persuasion; lessons based
> On fear are lessons rammed into the marrow.
> Indeed, is it not simple to remember
> That a mere hint of insubordination
> Shall cost a man his life, his silly life,
> Than wade through legal tomes for definitions,
> At best ambiguous, of Good and Wisdom?
> Once mankind is accustomed to the thought
> That in six days I can destroy a world,
> You can live free within the spacious circle
> That hems you in, and there devote yourselves
> To arts and crafts, to science and romance. . . .

- **A VOICE:**

The President of the Republic!

(*The generals rise and advance as if to meet someone, then return as if accompanying him; but the one accompanied is invisible. The invisible President is led to an empty armchair, and from the motions of* LUMP *and the* MINISTER *it is evident that they are seating him.*)

- **MINISTER** (*to empty chair*)

Mr. President, I take the liberty to say that you have arrived

67

at a most opportune moment! In the course of this one day an event of such overwhelming importance has taken place, that your presence here is indispensable. Mr. President, certain evidence obliges us to conclude that we are approaching a political coup d'état—or, more correctly, that this coup d'état is taking place right now, here, within this room. Incredible but true. At least, I, and the commission here, and . . . and, in a word, everybody present, feel that we must submit and accept the inevitable. . . . We are listening at the moment to a speech— I find it difficult to define it—but it is—Mr. President, it sounds almost as a throne speech. . . .

• TRANCE

All right, Waltz, on with the show. I'm filled with admiration for you. You're a genius.

• MINISTER

Listen to this, Mr. President, just listen to this. . . .

• WALTZ

    Oh, I can see you're anxious to partake
    Of this New Life! A ghost alone is free,
    But men should always feel a boundary,
    Material fences that affirm existence.
    Embellish them, conceal them with the bindweed
    Of worries and the roses of amusement,
    While I stay keeper of the garden key.

Mr. President, don't tell me you too cannot see the little clockwork car those people are sending back and forth across the table? You don't? I would have assumed that owing to a certain peculiarity of yours you would be just the one to perceive the invisible.

• TRANCE

Don't digress, Waltz. Everyone is sitting perfectly still, and there's no toy of any kind here. We are listening to you.

- WALTZ

And that music upstairs! It's maddening.

> (Trance *goes out*).

- COLONEL

It comes from the solarium on the roof. There's nothing wrong with a little music.

- MINISTER

Exactly, exactly. Go on, the President is waiting.

- TRANCE (*comes back; the music has stopped*)

It was General Gump's daughter offering herself to the sun. It's OK now.

- WALTZ (*continuing his speech which he now reads from a notebook*)

While I stay keeper of the garden key.

> (*Applause*).

- WALTZ

I shall take care of you, against my dream
Checking the pliable reality.
And Good shall blossom, and all Evil melt
Amid the radiance of my cloudless code.

> (*Annabella discreetly enters*).

- WALTZ

Here, Mr. President, take these notes and recite the rest of my speech.
(*They huddle over it, and presently Hump is designated as reader*).

- ANNABELLA

Hullo. Oh, hullo.

- TRANCE

We are busy, girl, run along.

69

- **WALTZ**

Oh no, let her stay. "Girl"—what a rare word, what a growl of delight. She was speaking this morning of enchanters and gazelles—Oh, I want to hear more. . .

- **ANNABELLA**

You stopped my music.

- **TRANCE**

She means she likes violent, neurotic, unshaven men.

- **WALTZ**

We had been interrupted, remember? A sudden curtain or something. I suppose I fainted.

- **ANNABELLA**

You must not blow up wildlife sanctuaries, you must rest. Here's a nice magazine. If you look at pretty pictures, you won't have bad dreams.

- **TRANCE**

The tactless virgin.

- **WALTZ**

What can *you* know about a man's dreams, doubts, demons?

- **ANNABELLA**

A girl can approach a closed book with an open mind.

- **TRANCE**

That's a promised kiss: open mouth and closed eyes. The hussy!

- **WALTZ**

Sh! My speech.

- **HUMP** (*in a brand-new megaphone voice*)
    The happiness of mankind is to me
    Dearer than anything. If its promotion
    Demanded that I cede to you my engine,
    Or break it, or blow up my little home town—

70

Oh, vile! That's a tape from hell, the bloated diction of a dead trumpeter. (*Continues by heart*)

    I would have done it. But to blaze with love—
    Such love for all mankind—and not to save
    The world? No! I began with you. Tomorrow
    To all the other nations I shall send
    The same command—and silence shall descend
    On earth. Please, understand: I can't stand noise.
    Pain, like a black wedge, here, within my forehead,
    Begins to jerk when there is noise. . . . I can't. . . .
    What do we do when tortured by a drum
    Thumped on by brats near their sick father's bed?
    Remove the toy! I shall remove it. Now:
    My first command: Gunpowder, all the arms
    That are on earth, shall be destroyed forever,
    So that old films of war, of rain, of trenches,
    Shall seem as quaint as pictures on a rock,
    The art of apes, the squabbling ground of scholars.
    Henceforth there'll be no noise—and those who must
    Settle a private score with an offender,
    Why, let them take a bludgeon or a bat.

This is the decree with which I inaugurate my rule. It will serve as a natural foundation for general bliss etcetera. I would like to avoid further mention of the Telemort's capabilities, and so, most esteemed Mr. President, it would be desirable that without any further ado you answered me right now whether or not you agree to begin at once the implementation of my will.

    (*A pause. They all look at the empty chair*).

• **WALTZ**

I assume, Mr. Predecessor, sir, that at the first hour of the Era of Hush proclaimed by me, you are expressing with your silence as best you can your agreement to my demands. Oh, she's gone!

• **MINISTER**

Yes, he agrees. He agrees. . . . Gentlemen, he agrees, and I am the first to offer my oath of allegiance. . . . I shall apply myself. . . . A new life. . . . The word of an old soldier. . . . (*he weeps*)

• VOICES:

Oh, yes, we believe you. . . . You're here among friends. . . . No need for formalities. . . . Don't take it so hard, boss. . . . Here's a clean hanky. . . . You should have a drink. . . . We would all like some refreshments. . . .

• WALTZ

The old man is inclined to tears. Old snow melts messily. Enough. Get up. The session is closed. Be kind enough to start your work. I'm staying. I believe there is no dearth of sumptuous rooms in here. . . . But I prefer your study, Mr. Minister. Colonel, go and give the necessary orders.

• TRANCE

> He has prevailed. Alas, my humble friends—
> Henceforth your day upon his night depends.

Curtain

Sets as in Act One. Waltz is sitting at the desk. His head is band-aged. Colonel *stands by. Ten minutes or ten months have elapsed.*

• **WALTZ**

No, I can't any more. Enough for today.

• **COLONEL**

Alas, all these are urgent matters.

• **WALTZ**

It is cold and bleak here. I never thought that a huge bright room could be so bleak.

• **COLONEL**

And besides the urgency of these matters grows as they accumulate.

• **WALTZ**

Yes, yes, I know. . . . Why isn't my little Trance coming? It's time.

• **COLONEL**

I consider intolerable such agglomeration and congestion. Instead of a brisk thoroughfare the life of our nation finds in your office a dangerous blind alley.

• **WALTZ**

All right, all right, but why don't you stop making critical remarks? It's becoming a bore.

73

- COLONEL

I beg your pardon, Your Demency, but I am only performing my plain duty.

- WALTZ

A sonorous title. From "demon" or "dementia"? You're rather a grim wit. If I keep you as my secretary, it's only because I am fond of paradoxes. And also because you hate your job.

- COLONEL

Anyway, I am trying to perform it. Even the Lord Himself couldn't ask more of me. What is going on *here*, inside, in my breast, is nobody's business.

- WALTZ

Particularly since that's not your breast but your paunch. No, I cannot work any more today, I simply cannot. . . . My head is heavy. . . .

- COLONEL

Your head should not hurt any more. The wound was a trifling one.

- WALTZ

Yes, but I think I fainted, and there's nothing more exhausting than faints. . . . Everything is so complicated and muddled, deliberately muddled. The wound I have forgotten, but the attempt upon my life—that I remember. By the way, a little command I just sent out dancing along the airwaves will be carried out in some twenty minutes or so. Let us hope that someone will inform us at once of the results.

- COLONEL

If you don't mind, I would rather not know about those doings of yours. I am not competent in telethanasia. But here, upon your desk, lies my poor country writhing in agony.

- WALTZ

Were it not for inert fools and alert knaves, the country would have been happy long since. In any case, you know, Colonel,

I have decided to attend to business only once a week—say, on Wednesdays.

• COLONEL

It is my duty to inform you that in the meantime the country is going to ruin.

• WALTZ

"Ruin" is a big word. Please do not exaggerate.

• COLONEL

No, Your Demency, I do not exaggerate.

• WALTZ

Nonsense.

• COLONEL

Nonsense? Bedlam in Parliament and battles in the streets? That's nonsense? Millions of unemployed—in result of your wonderful decree "Every rich man shares his wealth with nine beggars." Why nine, for goodness' sake, and where are your rich people? In their caves? In America? Entire detachments from the neighboring kingdom quite calmly cross our border here and there to see for themselves what exactly is going on. Good thing, at least, that they do not quite know yet how to react, and are only sniffing the wind, evidently puzzled by the fact that a strong and happy country should suddenly begin destroying its own military might. Oh, of course you're right, all that is nonsense!

• WALTZ

You know perfectly well that I have ordered our neighbors, as well as all the other states of the world, to follow our country's example.

• COLONEL

And how obediently your orders are being carried out! When our ambassador to Germany presented your ultimatum, the

Germans, without explaining their reasons, asked us to recall him immediately, and, then, without waiting for him to be recalled, expelled him themselves: He is now on his return journey—a pleasant journey, no doubt. Our ambassador to England was heard out with calm, but afterwards doctors were sent to examine him and the idea of a sudden fit of diplomatic insanity was so firmly implanted in his mind that he asked himself to be hospitalized. Our ambassador to France got off relatively lightly—his proposal set off a storm of jolly laughter in the newspapers, and our country has been awarded first prize in the contest of political mystification. As for our ambassador to Poland—an old friend of mine, incidentally—upon receiving your order, he preferred to shoot himself.

- **WALTZ**

All this is unimportant. . . .

- **COLONEL**

The most terrifying thing is that you have not even taken the trouble to acquaint yourself with these reports.

- **WALTZ**

Absolutely unimportant. A hint which today, in. . . . twelve minutes, will be given a certain kingdom should sober up the world at once.

- **COLONEL**

If such bliss as we have now comes to the whole world—

- **WALTZ**

Listen, what are you nagging me for? I tell you I'm tired and cannot spend the whole day reading idiotic reports. I'll do it Wednesday—so where's the harm? Or else, examine them yourself if you can't wait—I'll be happy to sign them, and *basta*.

- **COLONEL**

I shall be frank to the end. You have removed the responsibility for discord and decay from those who normally hold power, but you neglect that responsibility yourself. Without your approval,

76

nothing can be undertaken to end these fatal disorders, but allow me to say that you are incapable of grasping a single problem, that you did not even bother to find out what are the legal practices of the country you have selected for your experiments, that you don't have the vaguest notion of politics and economics, and that, the reading of documents, to which at the outset you devoted yourself with such appalling zest, becomes every day more repugnant to you.

• WALTZ

I am not obliged to study the cobwebs of an old regime. A demolisher does not have to know the construction plans of the buildings he burns, and I am a demolisher. Wait till I begin to build, and you will see how nice and simple everything will be.

• COLONEL

It's useless to speak with you. We are all only participants in your delirium, and everything that is taking place is the ringing and throbbing inside your sick brain.

• WALTZ

What did you say? Repeat that, please! Colonel, Colonel, you are going too far. I may get tired of you, Mr. Paradox!

• COLONEL

I am willing to be dismissed any moment.

(*The telephone rings*).

• WALTZ

Ah, that must be Trance. Tell him to come at once.

• COLONEL (*on the phone*)

Yes, Sir. . . . Yes, Sir. (*To Waltz*): His Excellency the Minister of War has come to see you about an important matter, regarding that assassination attempt. You should see him, of course.

• WALTZ

And I was hoping it was my Trance. . . . Oh, well—this cup too I shall have to drink.

77

- COLONEL (*on the phone*)

Mr. Waltz begs Your Excellency to be so kind to come in.

- WALTZ

You are right about one thing. The disorder must be stopped. But it does not follow that I must sweat over papers from dawn to dusk. . . .

- COLONEL

Excuse me—I'd like to go greet my former chief.

(*The Minister of War comes in*).

- COLONEL

Welcome, welcome. . . . Your hands are cold, your cheeks are like marble!

- MINISTER

Just a moment, dear chap, just a moment. No time for caresses. . . . I am in an awful state. (*To Waltz*): I swear to you, I swear. . . .

- WALTZ

What's the matter with you? Hysterics again?

- MINISTER

I have just been informed. . . . with inexplicable delay. . . . of the audacious attempt on your person. . . . And I want to swear to you—

- WALTZ

It is my private affair, and I have already taken measures.

- MINISTER

Wait, wait. . . . What measures? I swear—

- COLONEL (*to Minister*)

Please be calm, my dear Master, my unforgettable chief. Nothing threatens us for the moment. Yesterday, in the street, an unidentidee. . . . an unidentified de . . . de . . . de . . . daredevil—who unfortunately has not yet been caught, but who shall be caught—fired an air rifle at *him*, and the pellet only grazed his head.

78

- MINISTER

I swear to you by all that is dear to me in life, I swear and swear again that not a single fellow citizen of mine had anything to do with this crime, and that therefore this country is innocent of it—and, on the contrary, is grieved and indignant. . . .

- WALTZ

If I suspected that some local fool were mixed up in this, probably half the country would already be fine dust drifting in blue space.

- MINISTER

Exactly! I was horrified. . . . I swear it is not so. What is more, I have received exact information that the shot was fired by a foreign agent sent here by our neighbors.

- WALTZ

I have received the same information. I think that the guilty nation has already been punished. (*Consults his watch.*) Yes. It has.

- MINISTER

An obvious move! The schemers wanted to lure you into repressions fatal to us. Ah, I'm relieved. . . . Yes, yes, that's wonderful, they must be punished. . . . Whew! And you, my dear Colonel— oh, you've lost weight—you look somehow more mature. . . . Lots of work?

- COLONEL

Oh, my excellent, excellent Excellency. . . .

- WALZ (*to Minister*)

Don't pet him—He isn't behaving at all well. Here's something for you to do, Colonel—find out if there is news already from you know where.

- COLONEL (*to the Minister*)

Will I see you again? Just for a moment, perhaps? In the gallery? By the statue of Pericles?

79

- **WALTZ**

Forget about statues. Get going.

(*Exit Colonel*).

- **MINISTER**

He has really grown up a lot. And those new little folds at the the corners of his mouth. . . . Did you notice?

- **WALTZ**

I am not sacking him out of sheer mischief, until I get bored with him—and that will probably happen soon. In appearance he resembles a plump pigeon, but he keeps cawing like a skinny crow. Here's what I wanted to say to you, my dear Minister. I am told that various disturbances are going on throughout the country, and that disarmament is proceeding at an absurdly slow pace. I do not like it. All this is really your fault, and therefore I have come to the following decision: for a week I shall not go into these matters at all, but am placing them entirely under your jurisdiction. In a week you will give me a brief report, and, if by that time the country has not quieted down completely, I shall be obliged to punish it—and you. Is that clear?

- **MINISTER**

Yes. . . . It is clear. . . . But—

- **WALTZ**

I advise you to eliminate the word "but" from your copious vocabulary.

- **MINISTER**

I would only like to say that. . . . Such responsibility! There's no one to turn to. . . . Everyone is demoralized. . . . I don't know how I'll be able to manage. . . .

(*The Colonel comes in*).

- **WALTZ**

Well, Colonel? Glad tidings?

- **COLONEL**

I am a military man, war is my business. I enjoy a good cavalry

80

charge. But what *you* have done is not war, it's a monstrous slaughter.

• WALTZ

In other words, Santa Morgana has been blown sky-high, is that right?

• MINISTER

Santa Morgana! Their favorite city, the Benjamin of that benevolent nation!

• COLONEL

That nation has long been our enemy, I know. I know that they too would not mind invading us. But still I repeat—what you have done is monstrous.

• WALTZ

Your evaluation interests me little. What are the facts?

• COLONEL

Where once stood a splendid city there is now but a gaping pit. At first count the death toll is 600,000, that is, the entire population of the city.

• WALTZ

Yes, that ought to make a certain impression. That little scratch cost the cat dearly.

• MINISTER

Six hundred thousand! In one instant! . . . .

• COLONEL

The population of Santa Morgana also comprised about a thousand of our own citizens. I even knew some of them personally.

• MINISTER

Why, that's unfortunate! Sort of spoils the picture. . . .

• WALTZ

On the contrary. Look at it as a collateral punishment to *this* country for its muddle and sloppiness. What's the reaction there?

81

- **COLONEL**

Numbness, stupor.

- **WALTZ**

That's all right. They'll soon snap out of it. (*The phone rings*). That surely must be Trance. Enough government business for today.

(*The Colonel answers the phone*).

- **WALTZ** (*to the Minister*)

By the way, I don't like your uniform. You'd better wear civilian clothes. All those cheap decorations. . . . Or else, wait— some time when I have a free moment I'll design a uniform for you. . . . Something simple and elegant.

- **MINISTER**

These medals are the landmarks of my life.

- **WALTZ**

You'll get along without them. Well, Colonel, where is Trance?

- **COLONEL**

Unfortunately that was not your courier, but the representative of our unfortunate neighbors. He requests an immediate audience with you.

- **WALTZ**

They caught on quickly. And I thought they would begin by asking our friends the geologists about earthquakes and hurricanes. Remember, Colonel, you once proposed that?

- **COLONEL**

I promptly rectified my error and suggested that we turn to the psychiatrists for help. Will you receive the envoy now?

- **WALTZ**

I shall not receive him at all. A lot of good it would do!

- **MINISTER**

Would you like me to talk to him?

82

- **WALTZ**

I don't even understand how in hell he dares come to see me.

- **COLONEL**

He was directed to you by our Minister of Foreign Affairs.

- **MINISTER**

I'll be glad to have a chat with him. I have some scores to settle with those gentlemen.

- **WALTZ**

Do as you wish. Your scores are none of my business.

- **MINISTER**

And your instructions?

- **WALTZ**

The usual ones. If his country does not surrender to me by midnight I shall blow up their capital.

- **COLONEL**

In that case I suggest that you tell our representative there to begin the immediate evacuation of our citizens—a considerable number has taken up residence there.

- **WALTZ**

I don't see why they can't attend the performances. What does it matter? Anyway, do as you wish. Funny—how fast I have grown fed up with the words "ultimatum," "explosion," "punishment". . . . I keep repeating them and yet people only understand after the fact. I shall not keep you further, my dear Minister.

- **MINISTER**

We'll see to it right away. . . . Colonel, send him to me.

- **COLONEL**

He is in the waiting room.

- **MINISTER**

Excellent. I'm off. My dear Colonel, if you want to see me later—

- **WALTZ**

Shut up!

- **COLONEL**

There, you see my position!

- **MINISTER**

Never mind. . . . Cheer up. I anticipate no small pleasure from my conversation with His Excellency, the Hoch-Ambassador. (*Exit*).

- **WALTZ** (*to Colonel*)

If Trance does not show up before noon, I shall ask you to find him for me. I am changing your uniform too. Maybe we ought to dress you as a bull-fighter.

- **COLONEL**

My official duties include listening to your witticisms.

- **WALTZ**

Or a Neapolitan fisherman? A Tirolese? No, I'll dress you up as a Samurai.

- **COLONEL**

If I have not committed suicide it is only because the ravings of a lunatic are not worth my death.

- **WALTZ**

I think I have already forbidden you to refer to lunacy?

- **COLONEL**

As you wish. (*Pause*). Ah, what a cathedral there was in Santa Morgana! Tourists used to visit it, lovely girls with cameras. . . .

- **WALTZ**

In any case you can't complain that I have not done enough work today.

- **TRANCE** (*from outside the door*)

May I?

84

- **WALTZ**

Trance! Trancy! Oh, come in! Is everything ready?

- **TRANCE**

Yes, I think you will be pleased.

- **WALTZ**

I've been waiting for you with the greatest impatience. Ever since the moment I decided to move, this room, those maps, that shadograph of your late president have aroused in me boredom, distaste, and even, you know, Trance, a certain fear. Well, when is the parade of brides?

- **COLONEL**

Of course, I have no business to interfere, but permit me to ask, you are planning to move?

- **WALTZ**

Why, my dear Colonel, haven't I told you my little secret? What an oversight! Yes, I'm leaving.

- **COLONEL**

And where are you going, may I ask?

- **WALTZ**

Ah, that's the question. Geography is not your strong point, I believe?

- **COLONEL**

My attainments in that field are irrelevant.

- **WALTZ**

Anyway, you must have heard of a small island called Palmora, 800 nautical miles from your country's southernmost promontory? Aha! You don't know it!

- **COLONEL**

There is no such island.

85

D minus, Colonel. Palmora Island has been requisitioned by me. I sometimes even think that I chose your country to begin my activities in because it includes such a jewel. Mildest of climates, eternal spring, iridescent birds. . . . And just the right size for me: a complete tour of Palmora by car, along the coast road, takes. . . . takes how many hours, Trance?

• TRANCE

Let's say five, if you're not in too much of a hurry.

• WALTZ

Oh, I won't be in any hurry. I have long been pining for peace, for silence—you cannot imagine how much I love silence! You find there acacias, aloes, araucarias—in short, all the plants that begin with an "a"—But all this, Colonel, you will learn from any encyclopedia. Yesterday I gave the order that within two days the island be cleared of its population and of the villas and hotels where your retired shopkeepers used to bask. (*To Trance*). This has been done, of course?

• TRANCE

I'll say it has.

• WALTZ

Don't be upset, Colonel, I shall probably designate your capital as the capital of the world and shall visit you now and then— every three months or so, for a few days, to see if everything is all right. And of course you'll send me reports, but written in conversational style and, above all, without figures, without figures, without figures. . . . I shall live there in a palace—and this young lady here has just collected a whole staff for me. From my island I shall peacefully rule the world, but all the while my litte machine will remain where it is now—a great distance from here—not even in my own native country, which is also unknown to you, but in another, in the region of. . . . Look at that, I nearly blabbed it out! Fine thing that would have been. I noticed you both pricked up your ears, and now they have drooped again. Thank God, I'll never again see this desk bare its teeth at me. To Palmora, quick, to Palmora! (*To the Colonel*). Well, is my plan clear to you?

- COLONEL

It couldn't be clearer.

- WALTZ

Fine, then. And now I have things to attend to in company of my dear Trance, and therefore, Colonel, I shall ask you to vanish. And by the way, take all this stuff with you and get in touch with your former chief—I have given him full authority.

- COLONEL

The bungling dud, content with unsuccess, invites the better man to clear the mess. (*goes out*).

- WALTZ

Run along, run along. Now then, Trance, show me what you've found. Why are you looking at me like that?

- TRANCE

Your nervousness must be the result of yesterday's attempt at your life. Don't touch the bandage. Remember, I was the one to place it and therefore I am responsible for your health. Here, let me fix it.

- WALTZ

No, leave it. I've long since forgotten. . . . The hell with it. (*He tears off the bandage*).

- TRANCE

I am definitely cross with you today. How come you have so quickly cooled toward the grandiose reforms that occupied you such a short time ago?

- WALTZ

I haven't cooled at all. I simply want a rest. . . .

- TRANCE

Beware, Waltz—that is a dangerous path!

87

- **WALTZ**

It's none of your business. . . . Your job is to carry out my personal orders. Incidentally, tell me. . . . isn't there some inobtrusive way to do away with the Colonel?

- **TRANCE**

What do you mean, "do away"?

- **WALTZ**

I have no further need of him; he is an unpleasant man, and I'd like—well, in short, I'd like him to disappear completely— an accident—that sort of thing. What do you think, can it be arranged?

- **TRANCE**

Come to your senses, Waltz. I know what happened: You've tasted blood today.

- **WALTZ**

I'm joking, I'm joking, that's all. . . . Let him live. And enough bothering me with idiotic problems! Call those people in—where are they?

- **TRANCE**

Outside the door. I think you ought to see the architect first— yes, and, the chef.

- **WALTZ**

Ah, the chef, that's good. Let's begin. . . . I really am a little restless today.

- **TRANCE**

I'll call them in. (*He goes out*).

- **WALTZ**

And you know what else, Trance. . . . I'm beginning to think that perhaps it was a mistake on my part to have disdained a resounding title, and not to have had myself anointed for the throne in accordance with all the historical requirements— ermine, priests, fireworks. . . . Oh, he's gone. How silly! (*A knock*). Yes?

- DUMP (*The Architect*)

I am here. . . . permit me to introduce myself. . . .

- WALTZ

Ah, that's good, that's splendid. I'll give you a list presently of everything I like, and maybe you can immediately prepare me something tasty. You know, in my youth I used to eat atrocious food and practically always was hungry, so that my whole existence could have been defined by an irrational number—a square meal preceded by a minus sign. And now I want to make up for what I have missed. Before I take you to Palmora with me, I must know how good you are at cooking my favorite dish—a big steak with fried onions.

- DUMP

I beg your pardon, but you see, I—

- WALTZ

Or, for instance. . . . that rare luxury. . . . chocolate ice cream. . . . For some reason, during my sleepless, lean nights, in summer especially, I used to long for chocolate ice cream more than for anything else—so filling, so sweet, so refreshing. I am also fond of rich pies and various kinds of fish, except dried herring. Well, why don't you say something?

- DUMP

You see, Your. . . . Your Serenity, actually I am an architect.

- WALTZ

Oh—you should have said so right away. Silly misunderstanding. Made me feel like eating. Well, let's talk about houses. You have already been told what I require?

- DUMP

You require a palace.

- WALTZ

Yes, a palace. Splendid. I like enormous, white, sun-flooded buildings. You must build me something fabulous, provided with fabulous conveniences. Columns, fountains, windows as wide as the sky, crystal ceilings. . . . hot water. . . . Oh yes, and something else, an old dream of mine—a gadget. . . .—should be electric, I suppose—I'm no good in technical matters—anyway, you wake up, press a button, and your bed glides off and takes you right to your bath. And then I want all the walls to have faucets for all kinds of ice-cold drinks, clearly labelled. . . . All this I have ordered from Fate a long, long time ago, when I used to live in stuffy, dirty tenements. . . . it's best not to remember.

• DUMP

I shall present my plans to you. I think you will be satisfied.

• WALTZ

But most important—it must be built quickly. I shall give you ten days. Is that enough?

• DUMP

Unfortunately delivery of the materials alone will take more than a month.

• WALTZ

Oh, no. I shall mobilize the army, the navy. The mahogany and the malachite shall be delivered within three days. . . .

• DUMP

I am not a magician. The work will take half a year at the least.

• WALTZ

Half a year? In that case get out of here—I do not need you. Half a year! Why, for your insolence I ought to—

(*Trance comes in*).

• TRANCE

What's the matter? Why all the shouting?

• WALTZ

I give this scoundrel ten days, and he—

90

- TRANCE

Nonsense—just a misunderstanding. Of course, the palace will be ready by then—even sooner. We'll get Spanish workers to build one of those castles peculiar to their country. Do you see what I mean, Mr. Dump?

- DUMP

Yes, I do now; at first I did not quite understand. . . . Yes, certainly, it will be ready.

- WALTZ

That's better. See about the masons today. I give you a hundred trains, fifty ships, and three airplanes.

- DUMP

It will be done.

- WALTZ

All right. Go and start getting everything ready. Wait, wait— you've forgotten your package.

- DUMP

Scatterbrain! It's a clockwork toy I bought for my son. Want to see it?

- WALTZ

No, no, I don't. Under no circumstances! I beg you not to. Please go! (*Dump leaves*).

- WALTZ

Let us continue, Trance. . . . I have no patience for individual audiences—Let them come in a bunch. All these delays are highly annoying. And tomorrow I shall order all the toy shops closed.

- TRANCE (*at the door*)

Come in, gentlemen.

(*Enter Dump, the chef; Bump, the chauffeur; Lump, the dentist; Rump, the housekeeper; Hump, the sports instructor; Stump,*

91

the gardener; and Mump, the physician. They all wear identi-
cal black clothes, except that Dump has put on a chef's cap,
and Rump a black skirt).

• WALTZ

Well, Trance, tell me who does what. Who's this old fellow, for
example?

• TRANCE

This is Bump, the chauffeur.

• WALTZ

Ah, the chauffeur. A bit decrepit, what?

• BUMP

In compensation, my experience is colossal. Biographical foot-
note: when I was a small boy, my uncle Herman, a great prac-
tical joker, attached a diesel engine to my tricycle, after which
I spent two months in the hospital. In my adult years I was a
racing driver, and the only reason I won no prizes was my
extreme nearsightedness. Subsequently I worked for private
employers, and was at the wheel of a luxurious automobile
when our last king—may God be his judge—was killed inside
it, by a gunshot through the window.

• TRANCE

He's the best chauffeur in the city.

• BUMP

I have recommendations from many crowned and uncrowned
persons. Moreover, I have taken the liberty of bringing along a
small model of the car that has been ordered for you. . . . (*Pre-*
pares to untie a package).

• WALTZ

No, no—that's unnecessary. . . . Damn it! No, I don't want to
see. Trance, tell him not to unwrap it. You're hired, you're
hired. . . . Move over. Who's next?

- TRANCE

Lump, the dentist—a leading light in his field.

- WALTZ

Yes, indispensable. If you only knew what an infernal horror it is to wait for hours in a public dispensary, with that burning pain in your jaw, and finally to fall into the clutches of an unclean and clumsy fool. . . .

- LUMP

I do not believe in extraction, and my drill is absolutely noiseless.

- WALTZ

You too shall come to Palmora. And who is this lady?

- TRANCE

This, so to speak, is the housekeeper, the—well—Madam. . . . Mistress Rump.

- WALTZ

Really? Ah, yes, I see. Tell me, Trancy. . . . Gentlemen, don't listen—I must have a few words in private. . . . (*He moves away and holds a whispered conversation with Trance, who keeps nodding*). Well, that's great. (*To Rump*): I hope, Madam, that you will. . . . I mean. . . . Oh, never mind—later.

- RUMP

For more than twenty years I was at the head of a famous establishment patterned on the classical, ancient-Greek model. My charges were accomplished flute players. I even went around in a chiton myself. And how many amphoras were smashed during those years! . . . .

- WALTZ

All right, all right. Later. . . . Now is not the moment. And who is this?

- TRANCE

Hump, the sports instructor. Didn't you say—

93

- **WALTZ**

Ah, yes! You see, I myself am not very. . . . You know—privations, early in life, a narrow chest, symptoms of consumption, too much intellectual work. . . . But I have always envied the muscular types. What a joy it must be to jump higher than one's own head, or to knock out a giant with one punch! Yes, I want to follow a daily program of physical exercise. I shall have all the necessary equipment installed—mustn't forget to remind the architect—make a note, Trance. (*To Hump*): Can you jump from here to there, for example? Let's see you doing it. Why the silence?

- **TRANCE**

He is a remarkable athlete, but, unfortunately, he was born dumb.

- **WALTZ**

I want him to jump.

- **TRANCE**

He tells me in sign language that the floor is too slippery here.

- **WALTZ**

Never mind. Jump!

- **TRANCE**

Let him alone, Waltz—there's a time and place for everything. Let me now call your attention to this illustrious—

- **WALTZ**

No, I want him to show me—

- **TRANCE**

—to this illustrious horticulturist. He will create for you—

- **WALTZ**

I don't understand why I don't get what I want. Horticulturist? Why? I don't need any horticulturist.

94

- **STUMP**

My name is Stump, from "stump rot"—a fungus. I give the faces of my flowers any desired expression, joy or sorrow. Not only the petals of my roses, but the leaves as well, are fragrant. I was the first in the world to breed a blue dahlia.

- **WALTZ**

That's fine, that's fine. . . . Keep breeding. . . . And this, apparently, is the chef?

- **DUMP**

The Chef: Chef by the grace of God.

- **WALTZ**

Oh well, I have already spoken of my culinary requirements to the architect—have him tell you, I can't be bothered to repeat things.

- **TRANCE**

Next, I highly recommend this butler. (*He makes a vague gesture*).

- **WALTZ**

Yes, yes, have them arrange everything. Are there many more?

- **TRANCE** (*with another vague gesture*)

The king of librarians.

- **WALTZ**

I shall ask him to collect for me unique rarities from all the libraries of the world. I want a private library consisting exclusively of unique specimens. I think they have all been interviewed now?

- **TRANCE**

No.

- **WALTZ**

Who is left? That one?

95

- TRANCE

No.

- WALTZ

I don't know, I can't see anyone.

- TRANCE

You have forgotten the physician. This is Dr. Mump.

- WALTZ

Oh, very pleased to meet you.

- MUMP

How are we feeling today?

- WALTZ

Extremely well. Only don't touch me, please.

- MUMP

Appetite all right? Did you sleep well?

- WALTZ

I'm fine, fine. See, I have even taken off the bandage. What's the matter with you? I want you to remember that I am taking you with me only in case of emergency, so you are not—I repeat—*not* to pester me. . . .

- MUMP

Yes, of course, that's understood. If I ask you it's only as a friend. . . .

- WALTZ

Trance, I know this man!

- TRANCE

Keep calm, Waltz. No one wants to harm you.

- MUMP

Don't be afraid of me—I'm your friend.

96

- WALTZ

I know him! I've seen him somewhere before!

- MUMP

Just let me feel your pulse like a good boy. . . .

- WALTZ

Of course I've seen him before! I've seen them all some place
or other! This is a deception! A conspiracy! Get out, all of you!

- MUMP

We're very excitable. . . . If this goes on, we'll have to try
another injection—

- WALTZ

Trance, get him out of here! Get them all out of here!

- TRANCE

Yes, yes, in a minute. Don't shout like that. (*The interviewees
gradually leave*).

- WALTZ

What a nasty man! And all the rest are very strange too. . . .
I do not like it. . . .

- TRANCE

Well, are you taking those nice people with you to your. . . .
what did you call it—Palmin? Palmarius? Are you?

- WALTZ

I can't spend the whole day choosing lackeys. This is your job,
not mine. In any case I can do without a doctor. I know those
charlatans! Don't you dare shake your head. I am not a child.
All right, let's continue, let's continue. . . .

- TRANCE

I hope the next group will restore your good humor. Aha, I
see you are smiling!

- WALTZ (*coyly*)

Where are they?

97

- **TRANCE**

In the next room. Would you like to have a look?

- **WALTZ**

You know, Trancy, I must confess to you—in appearance, of
course, I am not a youth—and I've been through a lot, have
learned all the horror of life and so on, but this you won't
believe—I'm very, very shy. I mean it. And somehow it so happened that—you know, what with poverty, and the pauper's
habitual gloom—fastidious fancies and the heartburn of envy—
somehow it so happened, Trance, that I've never, never once. . . .
And now my heart is pounding madly, my lips are parched. . . .
It's silly, of course! But what visions, what visions I've had!
How my poor solitude sparkled! . . . . What nights! . . . .
Dreams so powerful and vivid, you know, that in the morning
it was even a little surprising not to find a single hairpin in
the room—Wait, wait—don't call them in yet, let me regain con-
trol of myself. . . . Listen, I have a request—you wouldn't have
a mask for me?

- **TRANCE**

What for? Are you planning a carnival? No, I didn't bring any,
I could not know.

- **WALTZ**

I don't want a Venetian half-mask. . . . I want something—how
can I explain—I want the kind that conceals the entire face. . . .

- **TRANCE**

Ah, that's a different matter. I'm sure there must be some here
in the closet. We'll take a look.

- **WALTZ**

You know, perhaps the kind that children put on at Christmas. . . .

- **TRANCE**

Here, I've found several. Take your pick. Santa Claus, for
example. Won't do? Well, then, this one—a grinning pig. No?

98

Ah, here's a nice one. Choosy, aren't you? What about this one?

• WALTZ

Yes, this one's all right.

• TRANCE

It's a little scary. Brrr!

• WALTZ

A face like any other. How does one put it on? . . . .

• TRANCE

How odd that you should receive ladies in that get-up.

• WALTZ

There, that's fine. Quick, now! Don't talk so much. Call them in.

(*Trance claps his hands, and five women saunter in*).

• TRANCE

I toured the country far and wide in search of young beauties, and I think my efforts have been crowned with success. How do you like them? Not bad?

• WALTZ

And this is all?

• TRANCE

What's that? I can't hear you mumbling through that mask. What did you say?

• WALTZ

This is all? Just these two?

• TRANCE

What do you mean, two? There are five here, at least five. Five first-rate little beauties.

• WALTZ (*to one of the younger ones*)

What is your name?

99

- SHE

Cleopatra. But my clients just call me Pat.

- WALTZ

Good God.... (*To the other one*): And yours?

- THE OTHER ONE

Olga. My father was a Russian prince. Give me a cigarette.

- WALTZ

I don't smoke. How old are you?

- CLEOPATRA

I'm seventeen, and my sister here is a year older.

- WALTZ

That's strange—you both look much, much older. Trance, what's going on here? And those.... what are those? ....

- TRANCE

Which one do you have in mind? This one? Cute, eh? The oriental type, wouldn't you say?

- WALTZ

Why is she so.... so....

- TRANCE

How's that? Can't hear you.

- WALTZ

Why.... Why is she so fat?

- TRANCE

Well, you know, not everybody finds beanpoles attractive. However, here's a skinny one for you.

- WALTZ

This one? But she's dreadful! Trance, she's dreadful—and she has something wrong with her....

(*The Fat One suddenly begins to sing, to the tune of* "Otoydee,

100

ne glyadee"—*"Go away, do not look . . ."*—*a Russian Tsigan ballad*):

• THE FAT ONE

(1)

There are lights in the dark,
And a ferry is there,
And the river is wide
Where we part in despair.

(2)

And there's someone unknown
Who is singing ahead.
How I held you, my own,
But away you were led!

(3)

And the fragments of light
That the ripple retains,
And the shouts of the guards,
And the clank of the chains—

(4)

All repeat in the dark
That my life comes to nought
As they ferry away
The daredevil they caught.

• WALTZ

Strange song! Sad song! Good God. . . . A wide, desolate Siberian river. . . . I'm beginning to remember something. . . . Yes, I know those words. . . . Yes, of course! . . . . *I* wrote that poem!

• THE FAT ONE

I also know some gay songs—not only prison ones.

101

- **WALTZ**

Please, stop! Please, please, no more singing!

- **CLEOPATRA** (*indicating the Skinny One*)

She can play the piano with her feet, and even shuffle a deck of cards.

- **THE SKINNY ONE**

I was born that way. Some amateurs prize it highly.

- **WALTZ**

Trance, she has no arms!

- **TRANCE**

You wanted variety. I don't know what you are grumbling about?

- **OLD BLONDE**

Me, I'm modest, I'm cultured. . . . I stand and watch from afar. . . .
What bliss to be in the same room with you. . . .

- **TRANCE**

She is a poetess. Talent, Bohemia. . . . In love with you from the very first day.

- **OLD BLONDE** (*stepping up close to Waltz*)

You'd better ask me how I managed to obtain your picture. . . .
Look at me: I'm yours, all of me—my golden hair, and my melancholy, and my hands, heavy with other men's kisses. . . .
Do with me as you want. . . . Oh, don't be lured by those pretty dolls—they are unworthy of your intuition. . . . I shall give you that happiness for which we both have been yearning. . . . My master! My cruel despot! . . . .

- **WALTZ**

Don't you dare touch me! Repulsive hag. . . .

- **THE FAT ONE**

Sweetie, come with me. . . .

102

- THE SKINNY ONE

Venus also was without arms. . . .

- WALTZ

Leave me alone! Get out of here! Trance, what is this nightmare? How did you dare, you scoundrel! (*Tears off his mask*). I ordered thirty young beauties, and you bring me two sluts and three hags. . . . You'll pay for this! You're a traitor!

- TRANCE

Run along, my little beauties. The sultan is not in the mood.

(*They go out single file*).

- WALTZ

This is sheer mockery. What good is such trash to me? I asked you for youth, beauty, innocence, tenderness, languor, peach bloom, fragility, grace, dreaminess. . . .

- TRANCE

That's enough, that's enough!

- WALTZ

No, it's not enough! Be so kind as to listen! Who am I—a travelling salesman in a provincial brothel or the king of the world with desires unlimited?

- TRANCE

I don't really know. That's a rather complicated question. . . .

- WALTZ

Oh, it's complicated, is it? I'll show you how complicated it is! This very day you will supply me with an album containing photographs of all the young girls in the capital, and I'll do the choosing myself. How dare you! Listen—here's an excellent idea. Not so long ago. . . . or perhaps it was long ago. . . . I don't know. . . . But anyway I did see her. . . . A very young girl. . . . Ah, I remember—the daughter of that imbecile general . . . So, then—see to it—Have her brought here at once.

103

- **TRANCE**

Look, Waltzy boy, aren't you a bit rude? I'm a very attractive young woman myself, as stylish and depraved as any morganatic wife.

- **WALTZ**

Get that girl.

- **TRANCE**

Not interested?

- **WALTZ**

No, Trance, no. Get me that girl.

- **TRANCE**

My potentate is given one last chance to enter this most pleasurable trance.

- **WALTZ**

Will you get her—yes or no?

- **TRANCE**

Ask her father.

(*Suddenly General Gump comes in, limping rapidly*).

- **GUMP**

Here I am! As you see, my gout did not keep me from coming—I jumped out of bed like a healthy man. Well, how are things? Crown comfortable, ermine not too heavy? Har, har, har!

- **WALTZ** (*to Trance*)

Inform him of my wish.

- **TRANCE**

It's a little embarrassing. . . .

- **WALTZ**

I beg you, Trance, *please*, Trancy. . . .

- **TRANCE**

104

Listen, General—where is your charming daughter, is she at home?

• GUMP

Oh, no! Certain tactical and tactful considerations have induced me to send my little girl abroad.

• WALTZ

Considerations, eh? You dare have considerations?

• GUMP

What a fiery fellow! Others complain but I like that cockiness of yours. By God, I do!

• TRANCE

It's no use, Waltz—give up. Let us change the subject. . . .

• WALTZ

I'll show you how to change the subject! Fine. . . . In short, General, be so kind as to inform your daughter at once that an aircraft will be sent to fetch her immediately. Where is she?

• GUMP

Come, come, my good fellow—why do you frighten me like that? My daughter has never flown and, as long as I live, never shall.

• WALTZ

I am asking you: WHERE IS YOUR DAUGHTER?

• GUMP

And why, good Sir, are you so anxious to know?

• WALTZ

She must be brought here immediately. Immediately! By the way, how old is she?

• GUMP

How old? Seventeen. Yes. . . . My late wife would have been fifty-two now.

105

- **WALTZ**

I am waiting. Where is she?

- **GUMP**

In the next world, as far as I know.

- **WALTZ**

I am asking you, WHERE IS YOUR DAUGHTER? I am taking her with me to my island. Well?

- **GUMP** (*to Trance*)

What on earth does he want of me? What island? Whom is he going to take?

- **WALTZ**

I am asking you—

- **TRANCE**

Stop it, Waltz, that'll do. You are not behaving well.

- **WALTZ**

Shut up! I ask you for the last time, General: where is your daughter?

- **GUMP**

And I have no intention of telling you. Har, har, har!

- **WALTZ**

What do you mean, no intention? I. . . . This means you have hidden her from me?

- **GUMP**

And how!

- **WALTZ**

Then. . . . Then, you refuse to deliver her to me? Is that correct?

- **GUMP**

My good fellow, you must have taken a nip too much. . . . Or, if this is a joke, it is in questionable taste.

106

- **WALTZ**

No, it's *you* who are joking with *me!* Admit it—eh? Why not admit it? . . . You see, I am willing to laugh. You *are* joking, aren't you?

- **GUMP**

Not in the least. I'm fond of jesting, and I admit it. But right now I am quite serious.

- **TRANCE**

It's true, Waltz, it's true! Something has changed! He really is not joking!

- **WALTZ**

Fine. Unless your daughter is here, in this room, by tomorrow— you hear me: tomorrow—I shall take terrible measures.

- **GUMP**

Take whatever measures you want. You will never lay eyes on my girl.

- **WALTZ**

Oh, my first step will be somewhat old-fashioned: you will be hanged, General, after extensive and highly varied tortures.

- **GUMP**

I have a weak heart. The program of tortures will be cut short very soon. Har, har, har.

- **TRANCE**

Waltz! General! That's enough, my dear General, leave him alone. Can't you see. . . .

- **WALTZ**

I shall take other measures, and shall take them this very minute. Either you deliver your daughter to me, or else I blow up your entire country—city by city, village by village.

107

• GUMP

I never understood the noble dilemmas of tragic heroes. All questions are unicorns to me. Blast away, my friend.

• WALTZ

I'll blow up the whole world. She will perish too.

• GUMP

This too I accept. You fail to realize one simple fact, my dear chap: namely, that the end of the world plus my own end plus the end of my daughter are a thousand times more acceptable than her dishonor—if you'll excuse the term.

• WALTZ

Have it your way—I'll marry her.

• GUMP

Har, har, har! You make my sides split, friend. . . .

• WALTZ

And if I am magnanimous? If I am infinitely generous? General, I offer you a million. . . . two million. . . .

• GUMP

You see, I told you all along that it was all a joke. . . .

• WALTZ

One right now, the other on delivery. . . . Or rather, name your own price. . . .

• GUMP

And a rather vile joke at that.

• WALTZ

I can't stand it any longer. . . . Where is she, where is she, where is she?

• GUMP

Don't bother to search: she is just as well hidden as your machine. Good-bye, Sir. (*He goes*).

- **WALTZ**

Hold him! Trance! It can't be possible that there's no way. . . .
Help me, Trance! I'll shoot him. Where is my gold-plated
automatic?

- **TRANCE**

You never had one, darling. Alas, the game is up.

- **WALTZ**

What game? What are you saying? . . . You are entangling me
in terrible thoughts, which I don't want to let in, not at any
cost. . . . You'll see. . . . No later than tomorrow I shall begin
such a reign of terror, such executions. . . .

- **TRANCE**

Waltz, I have encouraged you, I have gone along with you until
now, because I thought that this method might do you some
good; but now I see—

- **WALTZ**

Silence! I don't allow it! That tone of voice is forbidden in my
kingdom!

- **TRANCE**

On the contrary, I see that it is indispensable. . . .

- **WALTZ**

Get out of here!

- **TRANCE**

I'll go in a minute—I'm disappointed in you—but, in parting,
I want to reveal one little truth to you. Waltz, you have no
machine. (*Goes behind Waltz's back and disappears behind the
drapery. Already in the room are the Minister of War and the
Colonel the former immediately sits down at the desk in the
same attitude as in Act One, and bends over some papers*).

- **WALTZ**

Trance! Where are you? Where. . . .

109

(Goes up to the desk at which the Minister is seated.)

•   MINISTER *(raising his head slowly)*

Yes, this is certainly curious.

•   WALTZ

So you think this is all my sick fancy, that I'm saying it just like that? . . . .

•   MINISTER

Just a minute, just a minute. In the first place, calm down. In the second, try to understand what I am going to say to you. . . .

•   WALTZ

Oh, no—you wait a moment. . . . I know now what I must do.

•   MINISTER

Now I'll tell you: your invention, no matter how interesting and significant it may be, or, rather, for the very reason that you consider it to be so—

•   WALTZ

. . . . Stop, wait!

•   MINISTER

—cannot be the subject of such an agitated conversation as you take the liberty to conduct with me in my own office. I must ask you to. . . .

•   WALTZ

Very well! I'll show you. . . . It should have been clear to a child, a backward child! Understand—I possess a weapon of such power that next to it, all of your bombs are nothing—mere firecrackers. . . .

•   MINISTER

I must really ask you not to raise your voice like that. I received you in result of a misunderstanding—these matters are handled not by me but by my subordinates—but I still have listened to what you had to say, and have taken note of everything, and now I am not detaining you. If you wish, you may present your project in written form.

• WALTZ

Is that the only answer you have for me? For me, who can this very second annihilate any city, any mountain?

• MINISTER (*rings*)

I hope you will not begin with our pretty little mountain. (*The Colonel has opened the window*). Look how charming it is. . . . How peaceful, how pensive!

• WALTZ

You fool! Try to understand—I shall wipe out the whole world. You don't believe me? All right, I shall be frank with you: the machine is not somewhere else, it is here, with me, in my pocket, in my breast. . . . Either you will acknowledge my power, with all the consequences of such recognition, or else—

(*Enter: Hump, Dump and Mump*).

• COLONEL

He's mad. Take him away.

• WALTZ

—or else, such destruction will begin. . . .—What are you doing, leave me alone, I am not to be touched. . . . I might explode.

(*He is taken out by force*).

• MINISTER

Be careful, don't hurt the poor fellow.

Curtain

111